SEASON BY SEASON

The Sonoma County Farmers Market Cookbook

Compiled and edited by
Hilda Swartz
Margaret Terrian
and
The Committee

Illustrated by Kim Morgan
Cover design by Mary Ann Nardo
Cover photographs by Hilda Swartz

SEASON BY SEASON
The Sonoma County Farmers Market Cookbook

ISBN 0-9621329-0-X

Two Broads Publishing Co.
20 Eucalyptus Avenue, Ste. A
Petaluma, California 94952

TABLE OF CONTENTS

Preface   1

About This Book   2

Dedication   3

Paul's Raviolis   4

Spring   7

Summer   37

Fall   69

Winter   103

Canning, Preserving and Freezing   137

Index   157

THANKS

The Sonoma County Certified Farmers Markets and
the publishers would like to acknowledge the efforts
of the following people in the creation of this book,
and to express our gratitude to them:

Gaye LeBaron, for her wonderful introduction

Mary Ann Nardo, for her cover design and invalua-
ble help in other areas

Dana McIntosh, for her seasonal writings

The Cookbook Committee: Roancy Aubin, Helen
Crowder, Maria Hardin, Vanessa Henderson, Dana
McIntosh, Mary Ann Nardo, Ellyn Pelikan, Hilda
Swartz, and Judie Tiller (and their patient families)
for their boundless energy

The Vertigans, who put up with a lot

All of the farmers, customers, chefs and friends who
were kind enough to give us their recipes

PREFACE

If there is a thread that runs through time, connecting Sonoma County's past with its present and its future, it is the preoccupation of the residents with the land they live upon. This has been true since the rich soil of the coastal valleys proved to be the real "gold" discovered by the farmers from Missouri, Kentucky and Tennessee who came in the Gold Rush to find riches and stayed to develop an agriculture.

Transportation and technology have dictated crop changes in the 150 years since the first settler plowed his first furrow. The field crops that once dominated, such as grain and hops, have all but disappeared. The replacements -- vineyards and orchards, pastures and gardens -- have ensured Sonoma County a major share of the state's farm economy.

The great chefs of the 20th century knew the region well. They have described in superlatives our county's agriculture to food writers from all over the world. They send couriers for our lamb and poultry, our rare mushrooms, our miniature vegetables and edible blossoms. The descendents of the early farmers, more basic in their approach to cuisine, know there is no pie like one made from Sebastopol apples. Whatever words you use to write the recipe, it all boils down to a land that is by nature blessed.

Inge LeBaron

ABOUT THIS BOOK

Welcome to our cookbook! Within it you'll find a collection of favorite recipes contributed by the farmers, customers, and friends that make up the Sonoma County Certified Farmers Markets. The "Certified" part of the name means that everything sold at the markets was grown by the people selling it to you. And, honestly, that makes a big difference.

You want the best, we've got it. Life is too short to eat hard pink tomatoes and tasteless strawberries every day. Farmers Market produce is fresh. Not big-store "FRESH!" , which translates roughly as "PICKED TWO WEEKS AGO BUT NEVER FROZEN!!", but fresh, as in picked-the-morning-you-buy-it fresh. The produce that you buy in a chain store has often been raised not for taste but for durability. It has to be able to stand up to being packed, dropped, and shuffled between as many as three different warehouses. In order to achieve this, much of it has to be picked before it has a chance to develop it's full sweet flavor. Taste and nutrition both suffer.

What can you get at the Farm Markets that you can't get at a chain market? A vine-ripened red tomato, a sweet juicy peach, an ear of corn that tastes like a million bucks? How about unusual varieties, like purple cauliflower and tiny toy boy tomatoes -- AT REASONABLE PRICES. How about someone who appreciates your business and says so, who takes the time to smile and chat about how to cook the things they sell to you? Do you remember what that's like?

Farm Markets are great for growers, too. In a time when small family-run farms are being squeezed out of business by huge conglomerates and chain store corporations, selling direct gives smaller growers a better chance at survival.

There's a Farmers Market near you just about every day. They're held in Santa Rosa, Sonoma, Petaluma, Healdsburg, and Cloverdale. For information on exact times, days and locations, call (707) 538-7023.

We look forward to meeting you. Bon Appetit.

DEDICATION

"Whatever I do, I like to do it simply."
- Paul Mancini

Santa Rosa farmer, Paul Mancini, was a Sonoma County treasure and we will never forget him. For many of us Paul Mancini will go down in Sonoma County history as a folk hero because of his simple honesty, genuine goodness, and deep-seated compassion.

We loved him not only because of the beautiful fruit he grew but for his caring ways. Whether it was a farmer or farm market customer, Paul treated everyone with kindness and respect, showing the larger community all that is right with farming.

He believed the mystery of life is like a dormant fruit tree. It may look dead in the dark of winter but is miraculously renewed each spring.

- Tim Tesconi

Raviolis and Ravioli Filling

Paul Mancini

Aside from being a wonderful man, Paul is also a great cook. Here's a recipe for homemade raviolis that we had great fun putting together for this book.

PREPARE YOUR FILLING:

4 bunches of fresh spinach
1 small bunch of swiss chard
3 pounds of boneless turkey fillet (smoked is nice!)
1 medium onion, chopped
4 medium cloves of garlic, minced
a few sprigs of rosemary
1 teaspoon of parsley, chopped
1 package of dry bread cubes, or about half of a loaf of dry french bread, cubed
4 large eggs
1/2 cup of grated Parmesan cheese
1/2 teaspoon of poultry seasoning
1/2 teaspoon of cinnamon

Steam the spinach and chard together with a bit of water until limp. Drain them, reserving the juice. Set aside.

If you're using fresh turkey, cut it into small pieces and braise it with a bit of olive oil until just cooked through. We used half smoked turkey breast and half braised ground turkey and it was great.

With a meat grinder (yes, there's exercise involved in this too!) or coarsely in a food processor, grind together the greens, turkey, onion, garlic, rosemary, parsley and bread cubes. If you're using a hand-crank grinder, this is a good time to get yourself a little bowl to catch the juice dripping. Grind it all up into a large mixing bowl. Moisten it with about a half-cup of the reserved spinach juices. Mix everything together well.

Mix in the eggs and Parmesan cheese, sprinkle over the poultry seasoning and cinnamon and mix well. Taste, and make sure that everything's to your liking. **Yields about 5 dozen raviolis**.

MAKE YOUR DOUGH:

6 cups of flour
1 1/2 cups of warm water
3 tablespoons of olive oil
2 eggs
a pinch of salt

With your hands, mix all of the ingredients together in a large mixing bowl. Adding more flour as need- ed , mix and knead until it's easy to work with, elastic and no longer sticky (8-10 minutes with gusto!). Roll half of the dough out very thinly on a large well- floured surface. **Yields 2 1/2 dozen raviolis.**

MAKE YOUR RAVIOLIS:

Retrieve your filling mix. Place large tablespoonfuls of filling in a row, about an inch from each other, par- allel to the edge of the dough but a couple of inches from the edge. Take this flap of dough and fold it over the row of filling, pressing down all around the lumps to make sure the filling is sealed in. Cut the row of raviolis out with a pastry wheel and place them on a plate that's been floured or covered with waxed paper. Repeat this process until all of your dough is used up. If you have to layer the raviolis, sprinkle a bit of flour between the layers. Let them stand, uncooked, overnight.

TO SERVE THEM:

Bring a large kettle of water to boil. A few at a time (don't crowd them) drop the raviolis into the boiling water and boil for approximately 8-10 minutes each. At the same time, you can be preparing or warming up a nice sauce for them (try the ones on page 89).

Mangia.

SPRING

"Waking up on a spring morning to the sound of a laboring tractor motor was a way of life in Sonoma County. As I sat up in bed and looked out the window, not sure if I was still dreaming, my eyes feasted on a sky of white prune blossoms and the endless carpet of yellow mustard weed. The pungent smell of freshly tilled damp earth, sweet blossoms, and crisp green weeds will be with me forever."

- Dana McIntosh

Mushroom Bisque

Chef Robert Engel, Russian River Vineyards Restaurant

"My favorite elegant and easy soup. In many years only one customer was able to discern the soup's "secret" ingredient: clam juice."

1 pound of mushrooms, minced or ground
1 1/2 cups of cream
6 ounces of clam juice (a small bottle)
2 tablespoons of minced shallot
6 fennel seeds
3 cups of chicken stock
1/4 teaspoon of salt
a few grates of nutmeg
4 tablespoons of butter
4 tablespoons of flour
2 tablespoons of dry sherry
fennel sprigs, anise sprigs, hazelnuts (op-
tional)

I think a meat grinder produces the best possible texture for the mushrooms, smooth yet with some interest. The next best alternative is to chop them very finely with a knife. The next *easiest* alternative is to use a food processor, but don't over process.

Bring the mushrooms, cream, clam juice, shallots, and fennel seeds to a boil and then simmer for ten minutes. While the mushrooms are cooking make a roux by melting the butter, allowing the foam to sub-side, and then stirring in the flour. Cook this mixture over low heat five minutes, stirring frequently. Set aside to cool.

After the mushrooms have simmered ten minutes, add the chicken stock, salt and nutmeg.   Add a cup or so of this mixture to the cooled roux, stir smooth, then whisk it back into the soup. Bring it up to a sim-mer and cook for fifteen minutes. Add the sherry be-fore serving.

Serve garnished with sprigs of fennel or anise or a sprinkling of chopped hazelnuts. Yields 6 1/2 cups, or 6 servings.

(from "A Chef's Notebook", by Robert K. Engel, Full Circle Press 1987)

spring

Red Bean and Kale Soup

Al Perry

Al is a loyal customer of the Markets, and a very nice man. Here are a couple of his simple, delicious Portuguese soups.

2 cups of red beans
6 cups of water
1/4 cup of minced onion
2 tablespoons of olive oil
2 cups of fresh kale, chopped finely
2 medium potatoes, cut up
salt to taste

Wash and soak the beans overnight. Bring the water, beans, onions, oil and salt to a boil. Reduce heat, cover and simmer til the beans are tender. Add the kale and potatoes and cook until they're tender.

Serves 4 or 5.

Fava Bean Soup

2 cups of fava beans, shelled and peeled
4 cups of water
1 tablespoon of olive oil
2 tablespoons of minced onion
salt to taste
1 cup of turnip greens, cut up
1 potato, cut up small

Shell the fava beans, remove the white skin and open in half. Bring the water, oil, onion and salt to a boil, add beans and cook until tender. Press the beans through a sieve and return to the heat. Bring to a boil again (adding water if necessary). Add the greens and potato and simmer until they're tender.

Serves 4 or 5.

spring

French Salad Dressing

Diane Toso

2 teaspoons of kosher salt
1 teaspoon of freshly cracked white pepper
1/2 teaspoon of freshly cracked black
   pepper
1/4 teaspoon of granulated sugar
1/2 teaspoon of dry mustard
1 teaspoon of Dijon mustard
1 teaspoon of lemon juice
2 teaspoons of finely chopped fresh garlic
1/4 cup + 1 tablespoon of good tarragon
   vinegar
2 tablespoons of French olive oil
1/2 cup + 2 tablespoons of vegetable oil
1 raw egg (beaten)
1/2 cup of light cream

Put the ingredients in a 1-pint screw top jar in the order that they appear above. Replace the top tightly and shake well. Chill well before using.

Yields about 1 3/4 cups.

With the addition of:
1 finely chopped hard-boiled egg,
1 tablespoon of finely chopped chives,
1 tablespoon of finely chopped parsley,
2 teaspoons of finely chopped green olives,
and
1 tablespoon of small well-drained capers
this dressing is turned into a Sauce Vinaigrette which can be served with cold asparagus, globe artichokes, broccoli, etc.

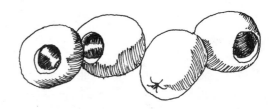

Crisp Sorrel Salad

Barbara Shumsky, Grower

Before using sorrel, clean it well. Tear off and discard the stem and center rib if tough; rinse the leaves and pat dry.

5 slices of bacon
1/4 cup of salad oil
2 tablespoons each of sugar and catsup
2 tablespoons of red wine vinegar
2 tablespoons each of minced green onion and parsley
3/4 teaspoon of Worcestershire
1/4 teaspoon of garlic salt
2 quarts of tender sorrel, washed and cut into bite-sized pieces
salt and pepper
2 hard-cooked eggs, sliced

In a frying pan over medium heat, fry the bacon until crisp; lift out, drain, and crumble. Set aside.

In a small jar or bowl, combine the oil, sugar, catsup, vinegar, onion, parsley, Worcestershire and garlic salt. Shake or stir until well blended. Cover and chill if made ahead of time.

Just before serving, shake the dressing well and pour over the sorrel; add the bacon and toss together until greens are evenly coated. Season to taste with salt and pepper and garnish with egg slices.

Makes 6 to 8 servings.

"How to use sorrel: Sorrel is good raw or cooked. You can use the tender leaves in place of lettuce in hot or cold meat and cheese sandwiches or hamburgers, or tuck it into a luncheon omelet. Keep in mind that heat will quickly fade its color."

spring

Fresh Green Salad

Brother Peter of Brother Juniper's, Forestville

This fresh, piquant salad blend comes from Brother Juniper's Restaurant and Bakery in Forestville, which also serves up some of the meanest barbecue around (our humble opinion).

THE SALAD:

Organically grown lettuce (3 varieties)
Fresh tarragon
Fresh oregano
Hyssop
Lemon thyme
A variety of greens, like mache, mazuna, russian red kale
Edible flowers, i.e. nasturtium, borage
(The amount of greens will vary, depending on the number of people you're serving)

THE DRESSING:

1 1/2 cups of olive oil
1/2 cup of balsamic vinegar

2 tablespoons of capers
2 cloves of garlic
peppercorns to taste

Puree all of the dressing ingredients and toss with the salad.

All of the greens for this delicious salad are available at the Farmers Markets.

spring

Asparagus Beef with Oyster Sauce

Chef Steve Ly, Peking Gardens Restaurant

This recipe is a great way to cook our great local asparagus -- it stays crisp, bright green and full of flavor.

12 ounces of flank steak, sliced into 3/8" x 1" x 2" pieces
6 ounces of asparagus, cut into 2" pieces
1 teaspoon of minced fresh garlic
3 ounces of onion, shredded
10 ounces of beef broth
2 tablespoons of oyster sauce
2 tablespoons of cornstarch, mixed with 3 ounces of beef broth
1 tablespoon of oil

Cook the beef and asparagus in boiling water for 10 seconds and remove. Heat the oil in a wok or saucepan. Put in the garlic and onion and stir fry for 10 seconds, then add the beef and asparagus and stir fry for another 10 seconds. Pour in the beef broth and oyster sauce.

Add the cornstarch mixture, a small amount at a time, just until the sauce thickens.

Serves 6.

Asparagus is a member of the lily family, like onions, garlic and leeks. It's been cultivated for centuries... the ancient Romans left detailed descriptions of the right way to grow it.

spring

Lamb Wellington

Chef Josef Keller, La Province Restaurant

1 lamb saddle
1/2 pound of mushrooms, sliced
1/2 onion, chopped
2 ounces of butter
2 bunchs of fresh spinach, washed
1/2 cup of red wine
3 ounces of liver pate
2 eggs
1 teaspoon of mustard
3 tablespoons of parsley, chopped
Worcestershire sauce, salt, soy sauce,
    thyme, marjoram, basil to taste
1/2 pound of puffed pastry
1/2 cup bread crumbs (optional)

Debone the lamb saddle, trimming off the fat. Set aside the meat trimmings. Tie loin and filet and roast it until medium rare. Saute the mushrooms, onion and meat trimmings in a large pan. Add the spinach, red wine, pate, eggs and spices, simmering for 30 minutes. Puree this filling in a food processor. Let cool.

Preheat the oven to 425° F. Roll out the puff pastry 1/8" thick. Spread with stuffing*, place the filet in, roll up and bake until golden brown, or approximately 20 minutes. Serve with Bearnaise Sauce (recipe page 58).

Serves 6-8, depending on the size of the lamb saddle.

*Add some bread crumbs if stuffing is too wet to stay put.

spring

14

Rack of Lamb with Herbs

Martha Baker Smith, Grower

Martha is a grower who sells wonderful dried flower arrangements at our Santa Rosa markets, and she gave us this very simple recipe for rack of lamb.

A rack of lamb
2-3 tablespoons of olive oil
1 cup of bread crumbs
3 cloves of mashed garlic
1/4 cup of parsley flakes
1/4 cup of rosemary
1/4 cup of thyme
1/2 teaspoon of pepper
a bunch of Dijon mustard (1/2 - 3/4 cup)

Coat the lamb with olive oil. Roast it at 400°F. for 20 minutes.

Mix the crumbs, garlic, parsley, rosemary, thyme and pepper with enough Dijon mustard to form a paste. Coat the lamb with it, reduce the oven temperature to 375°F. and roast it for 25 to 35 minutes more.

Serves 2.

Increasingly, people are re-discovering the fact that cooking with fresh herbs (versus bottled) makes things taste about a million percent better.
To keep fresh herbs fresh, try putting them in a glass of water in the fridge (like cut flowers), or wrapping them in damp towels, then storing in a plastic bag in the crisper.

spring

Glazed Lamb Chops

Rich and Saralee Kunde

Sonoma County grows some of the best wine and best lamb in the world. In this recipe, we use both.

6 loin lamb chops, 3/4 - 1" thick
2 tablespoons of honey
2 tablespoons of dijon-style mustard
1 tablespoon of Sonoma County Red or
   White Zinfandel wine
pepper to taste

Trim the excess fat from each chop. Score the remaining fat edge with a knife to prevent curling while broiling. Place them on a broiler pan. Sprinkle each with pepper.

In a bowl, combine the honey, mustard and wine for glaze. Brush the top of each chop with the glaze mixture. Broil the chops for 4 minutes, turn and brush the other side with glaze and broil for 3-4 minutes more. Don't overcook -- dried-up lamb is awful.

Serves 6.

If you can, make sure that the lamb you buy is fresh, not frozen and shipped in from parts unknown. It really and truly makes a difference in the taste, and costs the same, usually less, than "imported" lamb.

spring

Chicken Breast/Snow Pea Stir-Fry

Jeff McClure, Grower

1 full breast of a 3 to3 1/2 pound chicken
1/4 pound of snow peas or 1/2 pound of
  snap peas
1 medium onion
1 green pepper (or 1/2 green and 1/2 red)
1 tablespoon of cornstarch
6 tablespoons of oil
4 garlic cloves, crushed
salt and pepper
1/4 cup of sherry
2 cups of chicken broth (natural is best)
hot steamed rice

Slice and cut the chicken breast into bite sized pieces. Wash and de-string the snow peas. Peel the onion and cut lengthwise into eight pieces. Cut the pepper(s) into pieces about 3/4" square (discard seeds). Mix the cornstarch with 2 tablespoons of water and set it aside.

Heat 2 tablespoons of oil in a wok or curved skillet. Put half of the crushed garlic into the hot oil. Place chicken pieces individually into the pan and salt to taste. Turn the chicken as it's lightly browned -- this takes under two minutes! As soon as you get the last chicken piece in, start turning over the first one in. When all is turned, add the sherry, stir quickly for 30 seconds and remove the pieces to a side dish. Then...

Add 2 more tablespoons of oil to the **hot** pan and add the remaining garlic as before. Add the pepper cubes and stir-fry for 30 to 50 seconds. Add onion & stir fry until translucent. Salt and pepper to taste.

Remove those vegies to the dish with the chicken. Add the remaining oil to the wok and heat up. Add the peas & stir-fry 30 to 50 seconds. Add the broth, bring to a boil, boil one minute and add the chicken and vegies. When brought back to a boil, add the cornstarch mixture and stir 'til the broth is slightly thickened. Serve immediately over steamed rice -- delicious!

Serves 4.

spring

Fillet of Sole Sorreltine

Barbara Shumsky, Grower

4 tablespoons of butter or margarine
1 1/2 to 2 pound fillet of sole
1/2 cup of thinly sliced green onion
1 8-ounce bottle of clam juice
3 tablespoons of lemon juice
2 tablespoons of all-purpose flour
2/3 cup of milk
1/4 teaspoon of Dijon mustard
1/8 teaspoon of ground nutmeg
3 cups of finely shredded sorrel
lemon wedges

Melt 2 tablespoons of the butter in a large frying pan over medium heat; turn the fish fillets over in the butter to coat well, then arrange them in an even layer and sprinkle with about half the onions. Pour in the clam juice and 2 tablespoons of the lemon juice. Cover and bring to a boil, then reduce heat and simmer 3 to 5 minutes or until the fish flakes when probed with a fork. Lift out the fish and keep it warm.

Boil the fish stock remaining in the pan rapidly until it's reduced to 3/4 cup; set it aside. In a saucepan, melt the remaining butter over medium heat; stir in the flour and cook until bubbly. Gradually add the fish stock, milk, remaining lemon juice, mustard, and nutmeg; cook, stirring, until thickened.

Arrange 2 cups of the sorrel on a rimmed platter; top with the cooked sole. Stir the remaining sorrel into the sauce, then spoon about half the sauce over the sole and garnish with green onions and lemon wedges. Pass the remaining sauce in a bowl to spoon over individual portions.

Sorrel tastes a bit like spinach, but with a distinct lemony tang. It's been a staple item in French cookery for a long time.

spring

The Cleaned Out the Fridge Casserole

Elizabeth Gregson

1 cup of wild rice
2 cups of water
2 cubes of chicken bouillon
1 pound of ground beef
1 onion, chopped
4 garlic cloves, chopped
rosemary, oregano, thyme, pepper
any leftover vegies you have
2 cups of chopped mushrooms
1/2 cup of white wine
1 cup of light cream

Rinse the wild rice, add the water and bouillon cubes and simmer for 45 minutes or so. WHILE you're simmering, brown the ground beef with the onion and garlic. When halfway cooked, add rosemary, oregano, thyme and/or pepper (any or all) to taste. At the same time, add any leftover vegetables you have in the fridge, like corn, cubed potatoes, sliced carrots, zucchini, peas....whatever. Saute all until the meat is done.

Make a mushroom sauce by sauteing the mushrooms in a little butter until soft and stirring in the cream and wine until smooth.

When the rice is ready scoop a swimming pool in the center and add beef and vegetables. Spoon the mushroom sauce over everything and garnish with diced fresh tomatoes and green onion.

This can be made in advance and frozen. Just zap it in the microwave for 4 minutes, turn and zap some more, or heat up in a conventional oven at 350°F. for 20 minutes or so. Delicious with french bread and a crisp tossed salad.

Serves 4.

19

The Spinach Thing

Judie Tiller

The different tastes and textures of this dish are terrific:

2 large or 3 medium bunches of spinach, washed and coarsely chopped or torn
1/2 cup of minced onions
1/4 cup of chopped walnuts
8 ounces of cream cheese
1 cup of sour cream
1/2 cup of grated Parmesan cheese

Preheat the oven to 250°F. In small batches, steam the spinach just until wilted (don't overcook it). Layer it in an 8-inch baking dish with the onions and walnuts. Mix together the cream cheese and sour cream and spread on top of the whole thing. Sprinkle Parmesan over the top to cover completely.

Bake for 20-25 minutes (until cheeses begin to melt). Finish <u>briefly</u> under the broiler to brown the Parmesan.

Serves 6.

spring

Remember that horrible, soggy, grey-green stuff they called spinach? Not even Popeye could talk kids into eating canned spinach, and when you see the big crisp green bunches at the Farmer's Markets you think, "Who could blame them?"

Mustard Greens with Raspberry Vinegar

Pat Summers

A nice tangy way to serve mustard greens.

1 tablespoon of butter
1 large bunch of fresh mustard greens
2 tablespoons raspberry vinegar

Wash and chop the greens into bite sized pieces. Melt the butter in a large skillet. Add the greens to the skillet and stir-fry over medium high heat until butter is evenly dispersed over the vegetable. Add the vinegar, lower the heat, and steam for a few minutes, until wilted to your taste.

Serves 4.

Noodles and Cabbage

Tess Dancisak

A warm and filling entree.

1 small or 1/2 of a large cabbage, shredded
3 small sun chokes or Jerusalem artichokes, sliced
2 tablespoons of oil
2 cups of cooked noodles
2 sprigs or so of wakami*

Saute the shredded cabbage and sun chokes in oil in a large pot until tender. Combine with the hot cooked noodles and wakami and serve.

Serves 2 - 4.

Wakami is a type of seaweed sold dried at health-food or Oriental grocery stores. It tastes better than it sounds.

spring

Tiny New Potatoes with Fresh Herbs

Jean Reynolds, Jordan Winery

Small new potatoes (enough to go around)

2-3 tablespoons of butter
fresh chopped thyme, chives, rosemary,
    and basil
2 tablespoons of water or wine

Preheat the oven to 350°F. Wrap the potatoes in a double thickness of aluminum foil with the butter, a sprinkling of each seasoning and just enough water or wine to keep the butter from burning (about 2 tablespoons). Seal the package by folding the foil seams over several times.

Bake for about 45 minutes.

Potatoes are native to South America, and were brought to Europe by Spanish explorers. They were viewed with suspicion for many years (and grown for their flowers); Thomas Jefferson's neighbors thought he was a little loopy for growing so many of them to eat!

spring

22

Stuffed Kohlrabi

Zoltan Vasvary

The odd-looking kohlrabi comes to life in this recipe. The bulbous part that we eat is actually part of the stem, not the root.

4-6 kohlrabi   (about 2 1/2" in diameter)

STUFFING:

1/2 pound of ground beef or veal
1/2 pound of ground pork
1/2 cup of soft bread crumbs
salt and pepper to taste
1 teaspoon of paprika
1 egg
1 medium onion, chopped
3 tablespoons of butter or shortening

Peel the kohlrabi, removing and discarding the root and big leaves, and cut off the tops (save the tops -- we'll need them). Using a melon baller or a sharp spoon, scrape out their insides and reserve them, leaving a 1/2 "- thick shell.

Mix the ground meats, bread crumbs, spices and egg and fill the kohlrabies with this.

Saute the onion in the butter or shortening. Add the scraped out kohlrabi.   Place the stuffed kohlrabies in the pot neatly all about, cover them with their tops and add just a little water to the pot. Cover and simmer on medium heat for several minutes (until everything is heated through), then lower the heat and simmer until the stuffing is well-cooked, especially the ground pork.

Serve with rice, with a dollop of sour cream on top if you like.

Serves 4-6.

Kohlrabi is a member of the cabbage family that tastes remotely like a turnip, but milder. Ever tried one?

spring

Alicia's Quiche

George Hower, Press Democrat

George is a Food Editor for the Press Democrat.

1 cup of flour
1 cube (4 ounces) of butter, melted
4 eggs (or 2 eggs plus two extra yolks)
1 cup of whipping cream
a pinch of pepper
1/2 teaspoon of salt
1 1/2 cups of Swiss cheese, grated finely
1 cup of Sharp Cheddar, grated finely
Parmesan cheese (at least 2 cups)

Optional ingredients: (amounts approximate)
6 pieces of bacon, cooked and crumbled
1/2 of a zucchini, diced
1/2 of a crookneck squash, diced
1 yellow onion, diced
2 cloves of garlic, pressed
1/2 cup of Swiss chard
1 cup of mushrooms, diced

Preheat the oven to 400°F. Mix the flour and melted butter in a 10" quiche dish. Using your hands, spread this mixture evenly over the sides and bottom of the dish. Poke holes in the dough with a fork. Lower the heat to 375°F. and bake the crust until it's creamy gold - not browned.

Blend the eggs, cream, pepper, and salt together. Saute the onion, zucchini, squash, garlic and mushrooms. Cook and crumble the bacon. Chop the chard, cover it with paper towels and press down on it to remove as much water as possible.

When the crust is ready, sprinkle about half of each of the cheeses onto it and add about half of the filling ingredients. Pour all of the egg-cream mixture over the filling (don't let the liquid reach the top edge of the crust). Add more filling and cheese if there's room. Cover with Parmesan cheese until the egg-cream mixture cannot be seen. Spread 5-7 pats of butter around the top and bake the quiche for about 25 minutes at 375°F. Test for doneness before 25 minutes -- the quiche is done when the center is firm and it won't jiggle. Cool on a wire rack and refrigerate overnight before serving.

spring

24

Spinach and Ricotta Gnocchi

Ditty Cannard, Grower

1 1/3 pounds of fresh spinach, swiss chard
   or beet greens (about 2 cups cooked)
7 tablespoons of butter
1 tablespoon of minced onion
3 tablespoons of minced prosciutto or ham
   (optional)
1 cup of ricotta, lightly beaten with a fork
1/2 cup of flour
1 1/4 cups grated dry Monterey Jack or
   Parmesan cheese
1 beaten egg
salt to taste

Cook the spinach until wilted, drain and cool.
Squeeze out the liquid and chop it finely.

Melt 3 tablespoons of butter in a heavy pan; add the
onion and stir until golden (about 5 minutes). Add
the prosciutto and saute for 3 minutes. Add the
chopped spinach and saute for 3 minutes more. Put
everything into a large bowl and cool briefly. Fold
the ricotta into the spinach mixture. Stir in the flour
and 1 cup of the grated cheese and mix well. Add

the egg and salt to taste. At this point it can set for up
to 1/2 hour.

Preheat the oven to 400°F. Boil a large kettle of
water. Using a scant tablespoon for each, shape the
gnocchi dough into ovals about the size of a plum.
Reduce the water to a simmer and gently lower the
gnocchi into the water (don't crowd them). Simmer
until they rise to the surface -- poach for 4 minutes
total. Remove them with a slotted spoon, drain them
briefly on a towel and place them in a single layer in
a buttered baking dish. Sprinkle with the remaining
cheese and bake uncovered until the cheese melts
and the gnocchi are heated through. Serve pronto.

Serves 4.

"The gnocchi made with beet greens will be pink."

spring

25

Mustard Tart

Lucy Litman

"This makes a good appetizer. Serve warm in small wedges. It's good at room temperature and even good straight from the fridge the day after a party."

Pate Brisee (recipe below) or your favorite
   pie crust recipe
a jar of Dijon mustard
1/2 pound of Jarlsberg cheese
4-5 tomatoes
fresh parsley, rosemary, basil, marjoram

Make Pate Brisee (or your pie crust recipe -- roll it out to fit a 14" quiche pan).

Spread about 1/4 inch of Dijon mustard on the crust. This is almost a whole jar of Grey Poupon. Sprinkle about 1/2 pound of cheese over the mustard. Peel the tomatoes (dip them in boiling water to loosen the skins). Halve them and squeeze out their seeds, then slice them. Cover the top of the pie with tomato slices, making concentric circles starting at the outer edge, overlapping a little. Sprinkle with fresh minced herbs... I use maybe 3 tablespoons per pie

(less of dried herbs). Bake at 425°F. for 30-35 minutes.

PATE BRISEE:

1 1/3 cups of flour
1 cube of unsalted butter, room temperature
1 egg
1/2 teaspoon of salt
1-2 tablespoons of cold water (try to use the
   minimum)

Put all of the ingredients into a food processor and blend until it forms a ball. Remove. Form the dough into a plump disk, wrap it in waxed paper and let it rest in the refrigerator for 10-30 minutes. Roll it out to fit a 14" quiche pan. Bake blind* for 12 minutes at 425°F.

To bake blind: Cut a circle of foil to fit inside of the unbaked crust and cover it with dry beans or weights to hold it down. Partially bake, remove the foil and weights and finish.

spring

26

Oatmeal Raisin Bread

Mary Lucy of Lucy's, Bodega Bay

1 cup of rolled oats
3/4 cup of scalded milk
1 cup of golden raisins or apricots

1 1/2 cups of whole wheat flour
1 1/4 cups of all purpose flour
1 tablespoon of baking powder
1 teaspoon of baking soda
1 teaspoon of salt
1 tablespoon or less of cinnamon to taste
1/2 teaspoon of nutmeg

3/4 cup of oil
1 cup of packed brown sugar
3 large eggs
1/2 cup of buttermilk
2 teaspoons of vanilla
1/2 cup of chopped apple or walnuts (op
    tional)

Preheat your oven to 350°F. Combine together the oats, milk and raisins and set this aside while mixing the bread. Combine the next seven dry ingredients together. Cream together the oil, brown sugar and eggs. Mix well, about 2 minutes. Add the buttermilk and vanilla. Add the oat mixture. Stir in the flour mixture just until mixed. The chopped apple or walnuts may be added now as well.

Divide the batter into two 9 x 5 x 3 inch loaf pans that have been greased and floured. Bake for about 35 minutes, or until done ("done" breads, when thumped on the bottom, will sound hollow). Don't overbake.

Makes two loaves.

The smell of baking bread is, arguably, one of the best things in the world, or anywhere else.

spring

Rhubarb Crisp

Ditty Cannard, Grower

4 cups (about a pound) of rhubarb
1 cup of sugar
1/2 teaspoon of cinnamon
1 1/4 cups of flour
1 cup of packed dark brown sugar
1/2 cup of old-fashioned rolled oats
1/2 cup (one stick) of butter, melted

Preheat your oven to 375°F.

Cut the rhubarb into 3/4" pieces. In a large bowl, combine it with the sugar, cinnamon and a 1/4 cup of the flour. Transfer this to an oiled 8" x 8" baking dish.

In a bowl, combine the remaining 1 cup of flour, brown sugar and oats. Add the melted butter (cooled) and combine well. Sprinkle over the rhubarb and bake for 35 minutes.

Never eat rhubarb leaves, or feed them to anyone or anything you like very much. The contain a lot of oxalic acid and are quite poisonous.

spring

Chilled Strawberry Soup

Chef Kirby Tubb, Plaza Grill

A refreshing, delicious spring / summer "soup" that will knock your socks off.

1 quart of strawberry puree, strained
1 1/2 cups of plain, lowfat yogurt
1 - 1 1/2 cups of White Zinfandel (optional)
2-3 tablespoons of sugar (depending on the sweetness of your berries)

fresh strawberries or kiwifruit for garnish

Clean, hull, puree and strain fresh ripe strawberries to make 1 quart of puree. Add the yogurt, wine and sugar. Blend to mix and dissolve the sugar. Chill.

To serve, garnish with fresh strawberry or kiwifruit slices.

Makes 1 3/4 quarts.

Strawberry Rhubarb Frozen Pie

Bill & Ellen Adamson,

A cool and easy treat.

1   8-ounce package of cream cheese
1/2 cup of milk
1 jar of Happy Haven Strawberry Rhubarb Jam
8 ounces of whipped cream
1 prepared graham cracker pie shell

Soften the cream cheese, mix with the milk until smooth, add the jam and blend well. Fold in the whipped cream. Spoon into the pie shell and freeze for at least 4 hours.

Remove it from the freezer 30 minutes before serving.

spring

Sunshine Bars

Gene Merrill, Grower

"These are good with coffee, milk or tea -- they're great munchies and good for you!"

2 cups of dried apricots
1 1/2 cups of raisins
3/4 cup of brown sugar
1 1/2 cup of water

CRUST:

1 cup of flour
1/2 teaspoon of salt
1 teaspoon of baking soda
1/2 cup of brown sugar
1/2 cup of melted butter
2 cups of oatmeal

Mix the apricots, raisins, sugar and water in a saucepan; cook over a low heat for about 10-15 minutes. Let cool.

Preheat the oven to 350°F. Mix together the crust ingredients; you can omit the salt if desired. Spread one layer of crust on the bottom of a 9" x 11" pan; spread the apricot mixture on top of the crust, then put a top layer of crust over the filling. Bake for about 1/2 hour.

Let cool and then cut into bars.

California grows about 97% of the nation's apricots. Ounce for ounce, dried ones are higher in fiber and nutrition than fresh ones.

spring

30

Lemon Chiffon Cake

Lorene Tipton, Grower

Lorene is one of the nicest people you're ever likely to meet (and you can meet her at the Santa Rosa Farmers Market!). This cake is one of her favorites.

2 cups of sifted flour
1 1/2 cup of sugar
3 teaspoons of baking powder
1 teaspoon of salt

1/2 cup of oil
7 unbeaten egg yolks
3/4 cup of cold water
2 teaspoons of vanilla
2 teaspoons of lemon rind

1 cup (7 or 8) egg whites
1/2 teaspoon of cream of tartar

Mix together the first four ingredients in a mixing bowl. Make a well in the middle of the flour mixture and add the next five ingredients and mix everything well.

In a large bowl, beat the egg whites with cream of tartar until very stiff peaks form (stiffer than peaks for meringue, if you know how stiff that is). Don't underbeat. Pour the flour mix over the beaten whites, folding gently with a rubber spatula just until blended. Pour into a 10-inch tube pan 4 inches deep.

Bake at 325°F. for 55 min., then increase the heat to 400 and bake for 10 or 15 minutes more, or until golden. Cool the cake upside-down on a bottle.

spring

Avocado Chiffon Mousse

Bryce Austin, Grower

A serving of this smooth, creamy dessert packs only 243 calories. Try it!

1 envelope of Knox gelatin
6 tablespoons of sugar
2 eggs, separated
1 1/2 cups of milk
1 avocado, peeled and mashed
1/4 cup of lemon juice
a 9" graham cracker pie shell (optional)
whipped cream

Mix the gelatin with 1/4 cup of sugar. Beat the egg yolks with the milk, stir in the gelatin mixture and let stand for 1 minute.

Cook over low heat for 5 minutes, stirring constantly. Mix in the mashed avocado and lemon juice. Chill this until it's slightly firm.

Beat the egg whites until soft peaks form. Add 2 tablespoons of sugar to the whites, then fold this gently into gelatin mix. Pour into the pie shell if desired, chill and garnish with whipped cream.

Makes 8 servings.

Austin Ranch grows a wide variety of fruits, but is particularly noted for their 100-year-old apricot trees, still producing extra-large apricots.

spring

32

Carrot Cake

American Cancer Society

This cake is so-o-o moist that even if you forget to cover it (as we did) it doesn't turn into a brick by the next morning.

2 eggs, separated
1 cup of unbleached flour
1 cup of whole wheat flour
1/2 cup of sugar
2 teaspoons of baking powder
2 teaspoons of baking soda
1 teaspoon of salt
1 teaspoon each of cinnamon & nutmeg
3 cups of fresh carrots, grated
1/2 cup of oil
1 cup of orange juice
1/2 cup of unsweetened coconut, shredded
1 8-ounce can of crushed pineapple in
    juice
1/2 cup of walnuts, chopped

Preheat the oven to 350°F. Beat the egg whites until stiff peaks form. Set them aside. Sift the dry ingredients together in a mixing bowl. In a larger bowl, combine the carrots with the egg yolks, oil, juice, coconut, and pineapple. Add the flour mixture a little at a time to the carrot mixture, blending well after each addition. Fold in the egg whites carefully. Add the walnuts and stir very gently just until blended.

Pour the batter into a greased 9" x 13" pan and bake for 40-50 minutes. Cool, then cut into hunks.

We were pretty skeptical about the lack of frosting on this cake until we tried it. You may choose to ice it, but it's just as good without icing, and low in calories too.

spring

33

Oatmeal Cookies

American Cancer Society

1 cup of margarine
1/2 cup each of granulated & brown sugar
1/2 cup of egg substitute or 4 egg whites
1 teaspoon of vanilla
1 cup of unsifted all-purpose flour
1/3 cup of whole wheat flour
1 teaspoon of baking soda
3 cups of rolled oats
3/4 cup of chopped walnuts or raisins or a
   mix of both

Preheat the oven to 350°F. In a large bowl, cream together the margarine and the sugars until well blended. Add the egg substitute and vanilla and beat well. Mix together the flours and soda, then gradually blend this into the creamed mixture. Stir in the oats and walnuts until blended. Cover the bowl and chill the dough for about 4 hours.

To shape cookies, roll a slightly rounded tablespoon of dough between the palms of your hands into a round ball. Place them 4 inches apart on a baking sheet; wet a fork and press each cookie to about

1/4" thickness. Bake for about 10 minutes, and cool the cookies on a wire rack.

Makes about 5 dozen.

By doing a bit of substitution in this recipe, we end up with cookies that are high in fiber and low in fat and cholesterol, but still delicious

spring

34

Chocolate Walnut Fudge

Lorene Tipton, Grower

We grow great walnuts in Sonoma County, and plenty of them. Use nice fresh ones in this recipe.

3 packages of chocolate chips (the smaller-sized package)
a 7-ounce jar of marshmallow cream
1 teaspoon of vanilla
2 cups of chopped walnuts
1/2 pound of butter or margarine
4 1/2 cups of sugar
1 large can of evaporated milk

Mix the chips, cream, vanilla, walnuts and margarine together in a large bowl. In a saucepan, mix the sugar and evaporated milk and bring to a rolling boil. Cook this over low heat for 12 minutes, stirring occasionally. Pour this over the mixture in the bowl and stir until well-blended. Spread the fudge over a lightly buttered cake sheet and let it set.

You may find it helpful to post armed guards and large dogs around this fudge until you're ready to serve it up. Just a suggestion.

spring

SUMMER

"Warm summer evenings hurried the appearance of the first cucumbers, squash and tomatoes in our home garden. What a treat! Do you remember the old fashioned wooden ice cream maker that Grandma had? Into it went the sweet peaches just plucked from her back orchard. We took turns cranking the ice cream machine, waiting impatiently to taste the treat inside."

- Dana McIntosh

Giant Zucchini Soup

Althea Morgan

Two versions of a creamy soup which is light and delicate.

REGULAR VERSION:

2-3 tablespoons of butter
1/4 - 1/3 cup of finely minced onion
1-2 overgrown, monster zucchini, sliced thinly
1 regular can of condensed chicken broth, or the homemade equivalent
1/2 cup of half & half
1/2 cup of sour cream

Melt the butter in a large soup pan. Cook the onions in butter until soft, then pile in the sliced zucchini. Cover all with the chicken broth (diluted to package specifications) until just covered. Cook until the zukes are soft. Place all in a blender and blend until pureed, adding half and half and sour cream and salt and pepper to taste. Serve warm.

LOWFAT VERSION:

1/4 - 1/3 cup of chopped onions
1-2 overgrown zucchini, sliced thinly
1 can of condensed chicken broth (or homemade)
1/2 - 1 cup of plain lowfat or nonfat yogurt

Dilute the chicken broth according to package directions and place it in a soup pan. Add the onions and simmer until soft. Add the zucchini until it's level with the broth. Cover and cook until the zukes are soft. Puree in a blender, adding yogurt and salt and pepper to taste. Serve warm.

summer

Carrot Yogurt Soup

Terry Crowe

This recipe is great for summer, when carrots are rich and flavorful. It's low in calories and delicious.

1 large onion, chopped
3 cloves of garlic, chopped
1 teaspoon of curry powder
1 teaspoon of whole wheat flour
3 cups of vegetable stock (or homemade
**   chicken stock)**
3 large carrots, unpeeled & sliced
1 cup of nonfat plain yogurt
cayenne pepper

In a 3-4 quart pan, combine the onion and garlic with a small amount of water. Stir over medium heat until the onion is limp. Add the curry powder and flour; stir for about 30 seconds. Add the broth and carrots, cover, and simmer until the carrots are tender when pierced (10 to 15 minutes).

In a blender or food processor, whirl about half of the carrot mixture at a time with 3/4 cup of the yogurt until smoothly pureed. Add cayenne to taste. Return the soup to the pan and stir over medium heat until it's hot again. Serve with a dollop of yogurt.

This recipe can be doubled or quadrupled easily.

summer

Anise Greens Soup

Al Perry

Two great, slightly out-of-the-ordinary Portuguese soups from Al.

4 cups of water
1/2 cup of onion, minced
1 clove of garlic
salt to taste
1/2 cup of linguica sausage, sliced
2 cups of anise greens, chopped
1 potato, cut into small pieces

Bring the water, onion, garlic, salt and sausage to a boil. Add the anise greens and potato, cover, reduce heat and simmer until the vegetables are tender and the sausage is well-cooked through.

Serves 3 to 4.

Turnip Greens Soup

Al Perry

4 cups of water
2 tablespoons of minced onion
2 tablespoons of olive oil
1 clove of garlic, crushed
salt to taste
2 cups of turnip greens, chopped small
2 potatoes, cut up small

Bring the water, onion, oil, garlic and salt to a boil. Add the turnip greens and potatoes, cover, reduce heat and simmer until tender. Serve hot with Portuguese bread.

Serves 3 to 4.

Turnip greens have a nice bite to them. They're high in vitamins A and C, and have more calcium than whole milk.

Eggplant Soup

Chef John Ash, John Ash & Co.

3 medium eggplant (approx. 1 pound each)
2 medium onions, thinly sliced
1/3 cup of shallots or scallions, minced
2 cups of red bell pepper, seeded and
   chopped
6 cloves of garlic (or more!) minced
1/3 cup of olive oil
1/2 teaspoon of your favorite herb
2 quarts of flavorful chicken or vegetable
   stock
3 cups of diced tomatoes (canned or fresh)
salt and freshly-ground white pepper

Slice the unpeeled eggplant into rounds and lay them on an oiled baking sheet. Preheat the oven to 450°F.

Saute the onions, shallots, red pepper and garlic in olive oil until soft but not brown. Spread on top of the eggplant rounds and roast for 15-20 minutes or until the eggplant is soft. Be careful that the topping doesn't burn. It should be toasty brown.

Puree the eggplant in a food processor or blender with the herb and stock and tomatoes. Gently reheat and correct the seasoning to your taste. Garnish each serving with a dollop of creme fraiche.

Creme fraiche is what the French call their own fresh cream, which is thicker than ours and has a fine, tart edge. For a homemade version, add 1 teaspoon of buttermilk or 2 teaspoons of sour cream to 1 cup of heavy cream in a jar. Cover and shake it and let it stand at room temperature, uncovered, until it thickens (1 or more days). Ultrapasteurized cream takes longer to thicken than regular, old-fashioned cream.

summer

Wild Rice Salad

Lotus Bakery

1/2 cup of wild rice
1/2 cup of long grain brown rice
1/2 teaspoon of salt
2 1/2 cups of water

1/3 pound of sliced mushrooms
1/2 cup of almonds, sliced and roasted
3 sliced green onions
1 chopped bell pepper (green or yellow)
several sliced summer squash (green or
   yellow)

DRESSING:

1/2 cup of olive oil
1/4 cup of red wine vinegar
juice of one lemon
2 tablespoons of Dijon-style mustard
2 tablespoons of mixed fresh herbs
   (marjoram, thyme, tarragon) or 1
   tablespoon of dried
salt and pepper to taste
1 clove of garlic, minced

summer

Cook the rice in the salted water for 45 minutes, or until done to your liking. Cool and add the next five ingredients. Whisk together the dressing ingredients, dress, and serve.

Serves 6.

Wild rice isn't really a rice, but the seed of a native American grass. It's said to still grow wild on the edges of lakes in Canada, Wisconsin and Minnesota.

Summer Fruit Salad with Honey Lime Dressing

Chef Kirby Tubb, Plaza Grill

Assorted summer fruits such as:

Raspberries, washed
Blackberries, washed
Strawberries, hulled and washed
Blueberries, washed
Peaches, peeled and sliced
Nectarines, peeled and sliced
Apricots, quartered

Baby greens or butter lettuce
Toasted walnuts
Fresh lime slices
Fresh mint

HONEY LIME DRESSING:

1/3 cup of lime juice
1/3 cup of honey
1 cup of sour cream
1/8 teaspoon of lime zest
1/2 cup of whipped cream

To prepare the dressing: mix the lime juice, honey, sour cream and zest with a whip until smooth and creamy. Fold in the whipped cream gently to blend. Refrigerate one to two hours before serving.

Arrange the fruit on the washed and dried greens. Top with 1-2 ounces of dressing per serving and garnish with toasted walnuts, thin slices of lime and fresh mint.

It happens every summer... billions of berries invade Sonoma County, filling the air with their fragrance, only to be attacked by an army of men, women and kids brandishing bags, buckets, boxes, coffee cans and unbaked pie shells. Life's great, isn't it?

summer

Fresh Carrot Vinaigrette

Lucy Litman

8 fresh carrots, pared and cut in julienne
1/4 cup of water
2 tablespoons of tarragon vinegar
2 tablespoons of oil
1 teaspoon of salt
1/8 teaspoon of pepper
1 teaspoon of sugar
1/4 teaspoon of dried dill weed
1/2 teaspoon of fresh lemon juice
2 tablespoons of finely chopped scallions

Simmer the carrots in water until barely tender(a minute!). Remove from the heat and drain immediately.

Combine the remaining ingredients in a large bowl. Add the carrots and mix well. Cover and chill several hours before serving.

Variation: Use wine vinegar instead of tarragon vinegar and marjoram instead of dill. Delicious.

summer

Cucumber Salad

Paula Mune, Rocky Creek Gardens

A cool, tangy summer salad:

6 cups of thinly sliced cucumbers (leave strips of green when you peel)
sliced tomatoes and red onions for garnish

DRESSING:

1 cup of Japanese rice vinegar
1/2 cup (more or less) of sugar
   (if you use sweetened rice vinegar, omit the sugar)
Juice of half of a lemon
2 teaspoons of finely chopped ginger root
1/2 teaspoon of salt

Mix the dressing ingredients well, pour over the cukes, garnish and chill before serving.

"Is it fresh? Is it fresh? Picked this morning"

—Paula Mune

Lapin Gravenstein

Chez Jano

There are quite a number of rabbit growers in Sonoma County who can provide fresh local rabbit for this dish. To find them, consult the map published by Farm Trails* or contact the Farm & Home Advisor, Sonoma County Agriculture Department. The growers can also give helpful tips on deboning.

1 pound of Gravenstein apples
2 rabbits, deboned*, cut up into 8 pieces
each
1/4 cup of oil
1 pint of apple juice
1/2 pint of whipping cream
1/4 cup of lemon juice
1 pinch of salt
1 pinch of pepper
1/4 teaspoon of nutmeg
3 tablespoons of butter

Peel and slice the apples. Saute the cut up rabbit in hot oil in an ovenproof pan until brown; add the apple slices and saute them both together for a few minutes until the apples start to turn brown. Add the apple juice, cream, lemon juice, salt, pepper, nutmeg and butter, and bring to a boil. Cover the dish, place it in the oven at 350° F. and bake for approximately 1 hour. Remove and check the rabbit to make sure that it is cooked through, then place rabbit pieces on a serving dish. Reduce the broth to a medium consistency, then pour over the rabbit and serve.

Serves 8.

*The Farm Trails map is a great way to locate all kinds of fresh local products you may not find at the Farm Markets. Send a self-addressed stamped envelope to Sonoma County Farm Trails, P.O. Box 6032, Santa Rosa, CA 95406, or to your local Chamber of Commerce.

summer

Grilled Sonoma Lamb Chops with Bagnat

Jean Reynolds, Jordan Winery

8 loin lamb chops

MARINADE:
4 tablespoons of olive oil
1 cup Sonoma County Cabernet Sauvignon
2 cloves of garlic, chopped
1 onion, sliced
2 tablespoons of fresh chopped herbs
   (rosemary, sage, thyme, parsley)

Mix the marinade ingredients together well and marinate the lamb chops in it for 2 hours in a glass or stainless steel container. Wipe the marinade from the chops and grill them over hot coals until medium rare. Serve with Bagnat (recipe follows).
Serves 8.

BAGNAT   (Piedmontese Salsa Verde)

Bagnat is quick and simple to prepare, and great for meat, poultry and fish. This is my version of the sauce used on the famous Bollito Mistos of Northern Italy. Don't let the anchovies deter those who can't normally eat them. Their flavor, though not dominant, is essential to the success of this sauce.

2 bunches of Italian parsley, stems removed, coarsely chopped
3-4 cloves of garlic, finely minced
6-8 fillets of anchovy, minced
4 tablespoons of diced sun-dried tomatoes
   (in oil) or 4 tablespoons diced pimentos
3 tablespoons of Balsamic vinegar
3/4 cup of virgin olive oil
**salt and freshly ground black pepper to
   taste**

Put all of the ingredients, except the oil, vinegar, salt & pepper, into a stainless steel bowl. Stir in the olive oil until the sauce is flavorful but not runny. Season with salt and pepper to taste. Add the vinegar about half an hour before serving - this insures a rich green color. This sauce will keep for a week in a sealed jar in the refrigerator, but is usually consumed long before. Makes 2 cups.

Summer

Fish Fillets with Creamed Spinach, Chard or Sorrel

Simon Corwin, Lucky Duck Farms

1 tablespoon of unsalted butter
2 6-ounce fillets of red snapper or rock cod
2 bunches of spinach, chard or sorrel,
   washed and chopped
4 tablespoons of flour
2 cups of milk
salt and pepper to taste
ground nutmeg   (optional)

Melt 1 teaspoon of the butter in a large saute pan and briefly cook the fish on each side (about 1 minute each side). Remove it from the pan and keep warm.

Melt the remaining 2 teaspoons of butter in the saute pan and add the chopped greens. Stir until wilted. Sprinkle in the flour and stir until blended. Add the 2 cups of milk, salt and pepper to taste, and nutmeg if desired to taste. Continue cooking and stirring until it begins to thicken, about 5-10 minutes.

Add the fish back to the pan and cook until done, turning once. Serve over hot steamed rice.

Serves 2.

Simon is a (woman) farmer who grows unique varieties of lettuce and sells to local restaurants and markets.

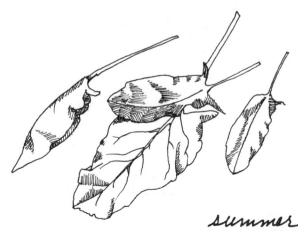

summer

Barbecued Salmon Fillets

Pete Petersen, Grower

4 large or 8 small salmon fillets

MARINADE:

2 tablespoons of chopped parsley
2 tablespoons of chopped shallots
2 tablespoons of olive oil
2 cloves of garlic, pressed
1 teaspoon of pepper

Mix the marinade and spoon it over the salmon fillets at least an hour before cooking.

Barbecue them skin down over hot coals for 15 minutes; turn and grill 10 minutes more.

Serves 4.

summer

Sauteed Mushrooms

Pete Petersen, Grower

1 pound of fresh mushrooms
1 tablespoon of soy sauce
1 tablespoon of dry sherry
1 tablespoon of parsley, chopped
1 teaspoon of flavor crystals (beef or chicken bouillon)
2 tablespoons of olive oil

If your mushrooms are large, cut them into quarters. Mix the other ingredients well and marinate the mushrooms for an hour in the mix. Cook them in a small frying pan, covered, for 4 minutes, stirring frequently. Add salt and pepper to taste, and serve.

For an interesting experience, try visiting a mushroom grower. The strange sights and earthy smells -- creating an almost eerie environment --- will stay with you for a while.

Salmon Saute in Blue Cornmeal with Salsa Cruda

Lisa Hemenway, Hemenway Restaurant

1-1/2 pounds of salmon fillet
blue corn meal for dredging
1/2 cup of clarified butter (for saute)

SALSA CRUDA:

medley of toy boy tomatoes (3 cups)
1 torpedo onion, chopped
2 cloves of garlic, minced
1/4 cup of capers
2 tablespoons of virgin olive oil
1/2 cup of pure olive oil
1 lemon
1 lime
black pepper and salt

Mesclun greens

Portion salmon into 2-ounce strips and dredge them in cornmeal. Let them rest for a few minutes.

Chop the medley of tomatoes and onions and toss with the garlic, capers, olive oil, lemon juice, lime juice, pepper and salt.

Saute the salmon in clarified butter until crisp. Arrange the Mesclun greens on plates. Lay two pieces of salmon over the greens and top them with salsa cruda.

This dish may be served as a first course or as an entree depending on the amount of salmon served.

Serves 4-6.

"Mesclun" means a mix or melange, and mesclun greens are a toss of wild and cultivated baby greens, including (but not limited to) infant dandelion, arugula, chervil, radicchio and tiny loose-leaf lettuces.

summer

Quenelles of Salmon & Sauce Vin Blanc

Jurgen K.A. Wiese, California Master Chef

3 pounds of boneless fresh filet of salmon
5 egg whites
2 1/2 pints of heavy cream
cayenne pepper
salt
white wine
clam juice

Grind the salmon 6 times through the finest (1/16")
setting of a meat grinder.   Place it in a bowl which is
bedded in shaved ice. Add 5 raw egg whites, one at
a time, stirring constantly. Pouring slowly, stir in the
2 1/2 pints of cream. Season to taste with salt and
cayenne pepper. With a soup spoon, form it into
balls shaped like small eggs and place them in a
buttered pan. Add just enough white wine and fish
stock (or clam juice) to cover the bottom of your pan.
Poach the salmon in the oven at 350 for approximately 15 minutes. Serve with rice, white wine
sauce and vegetables of your choice.

Serves 6-8.

SAUCE VIN BLANC / WHITE WINE SAUCE
FOR FISH:

3 cups of fish stock or clam juice
1 cup of dry white wine
1 cup of heavy cream
1 lemon
salt and tabasco to taste
roux (see page 8)

Reduce the fish stock by a third over medium heat.
Add the white wine and bring the mixture to a boil.
Thicken with roux, a bit at a time, to the sauce thickness you desire. Let simmer for approximately 15
minutes. Add the heavy cream; let simmer for another 10 minutes. Season with salt, tabasco and lemon
to taste. Strain through a fine wire mesh sieve before serving.

Summer

Vegetable Burritos

Judie Tiller

2 tablespoons of vegetable oil
1 large onion, thinly sliced
2 cloves of garlic, minced or pressed
1/2 pound of mushrooms, sliced
1 large green pepper, cut into thin strips
2 medium-sized carrots, thinly sliced
4 medium-sized zucchini, cut in 1/2" slices
2 large tomatoes, peeled and coarsely
   chopped
1 can of diced green chilis (drained) or 3-4
   fresh Anaheim chilis, chopped
1/2 cup of sliced black olives
1 teaspoon of chili powder
1/2 teaspoon of salt
1/2 teaspoon of ground cumin
1 tablespoon of oregano
1/2 pound each of Jack and Cheddar
   cheese, shredded

Pour about 2 tablespoons of oil into a 12-inch frying pan. On medium-high heat, add the onion and garlic and saute until the onion is limp. Add all of the remaining ingredients except the cheeses. Bring to a boil, lower the heat, cover and simmer until the vegies are barely tender when pierced, about 5 - 7 minutes. Uncover and gently boil, stirring occasionally, until all of the liquid has evaporated and the vegies are tender, about another 5 - 7 minutes. (If they get tender and the liquid hasn't evaporated, pour it off).

Stir half of each kind of cheese into the vegetables. Turn into a shallow ovenproof casserole and sprinkle with the remaining cheese. Place about 6" from the heat and broil just until cheese is melted and bubbly, about 3 minutes. Serve with warm flour tortillas, red or green taco sauce (optional), sunflower seeds, guacamole, sour cream, sliced green onions or other condiments. Eat burrito-style, or enchilada-style with sour cream or guacamole on top.

Serves 6-8.

Everybody will like these. They're easy to make and they taste great.

Summer

Zucchini Lasagna

Larry & Angie Rogers

3 pounds of fresh zucchini (about 12 small)
4 cups of dry bread
2 eggs
1/2 teaspoon   of pepper
1/2 teaspoon of salt (optional)
1 teaspoon of garlic powder
4 pounds of longhorn style cheese
1/3 cup of chopped parsley
4 cups of Italian pasta sauce with or without meat (try our pasta sauces, page 89)
1/2 cup of grated Parmesan cheese

Preheat your oven to 350°F.

Shred the zucchini and crumble the bread. Beat the
eggs lightly with pepper, salt and garlic powder. Mix
all of the ingredients except the Parmesan cheese
with pasta sauce. Put everything into a 3 quart baking dish and top with Parmesan cheese. Bake for
one hour.

Serves 8.

*One of the few lasagna recipes
without pasta (try it! its good!).
Remember, you read it here first.*

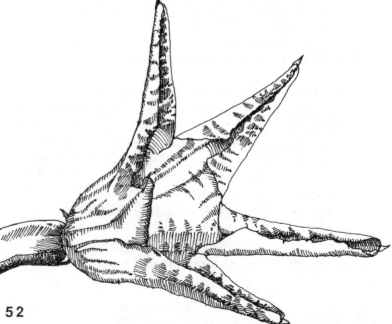

summer

Stuffed Zucchini

Margaret Fingerson

1/2 cup of brown rice
4 medium fresh zucchini
2 tablespoons of butter
1/4 cup of chopped onion
1/4 pound of chopped fresh mushrooms
1 fresh tomato, chopped
2 tablespoons of chopped fresh parsley
1/4 teaspoon of fresh basil
1/4 teaspoon of thyme
3/4 teaspoon of salt
2 tablespoons of grated cheese

Cook the rice as directed on your rice package. Cut the zucchini lengthwise and scoop out the centers to leave 1/4" shell. Chop up the pulp. Melt the butter in a skillet; add the onion and mushrooms and saute for a couple of minutes. Add the zucchini pulp and tomato and cook ten minutes on medium heat. Add parsley, basil, thyme and 1/4 teaspoon salt. Stir into the brown rice (or stir the rice into the vegies!).

Preheat your oven to 350°F. Sprinkle the zucchini shells with 1/2 teaspoon of salt and fill them with the rice-vegetable mixture. Put them into a greased baking dish, cover tightly and bake for 20 minutes. Sprinkle with cheese and rebake, uncovered, until the cheese melts.

Serves 2-4.

" The best place to be on Saturday morning is the Farmers Market."
— Pete Petersen

summer

Zucchini Pancakes

Laure Reichek

4 zucchini, coarsely grated
1/2 onion, chopped
1 clove of garlic, chopped
2 beaten eggs
2 teaspoons of flour
a sprinkling of chopped parsley
5 teaspoons of olive oil
grated Parmesan cheese (optional)

Put the grated zucchini into a colander and sprinkle with salt. Let it stand for an hour, then squeeze all of the water out of it with your hands, a small handful at a time. In a mixing bowl, combine the zucchini pulp with the onion, garlic, eggs, flour, and a sprinkling of parsley.

Heat the oil in a skillet. Drop large-serving-spoon-sized amounts of batter into the hot oil, flatten them with a spatula and fry until golden brown on both sides. Drain on paper towels.

You may serve these around a roast or a chicken, or alone as lunch or a snack. They're great sprinkled with Parmesan cheese.

By now you've probably suspected that we grow a lot of zucchini in these parts... try visiting the Farmers Markets during spring or summer and asking when the next Zucchini Car Races are going to be held (yes, we're serious).

Summer

Zucchini Pie

Ray & JoAnne Fishman

Delicious hot or cold!

2 eggs
1/2 cup of sour cream
1/2 - 3/4 cup of mustard, any kind, plain or fancy
1 large pie shell (if ready-made, thawed)
1 large onion, diced
6-8 medium zucchini, sliced thinly
2 tablespoons of butter
dill, salt and pepper to taste
2 cups of cheese (Cheddar, Jack or a combination), shredded
diced tomatoes (optional)
chopped olives (optional)
mushrooms (optional)

Beat the eggs well with the sour cream; set aside. Spread mustard generously over the pie shell; set aside.

Saute the onion and zucchini in the butter and spices (to taste) until tender and the onions are clear.

Put the vegies into a mixing bowl and add the egg mixture, half of the cheese, tomatoes, olives, and mushrooms. Mix well, but gently.

Preheat your oven to 350°F. Pour the filling into the prepared pie shell, then cover with the other half of the cheese.

Bake uncovered for 30 to 45 minutes, or until set and golden to your taste.

Serves 6.

summer

Grilled Polenta with Fontina Cheese, Shiitake Mushrooms & Sundried Tomatoes

Chef John Ash, John Ash & Co.

4 cups of water
salt and pepper to taste
2 teaspoons of ground white pepper
1 teaspoon of fresh thyme or oregano (or
   half as much of dry)
1 cup of polenta or yellow corn meal
1/2 cup of mushrooms, minced
1/2 cup of green onions, minced
1/4 pound (1 stick) of butter
1/2 cup of dry white wine
1 tablespoon of minced fresh parsley

GARNISH:

several slices of fontina cheese
shiitake mushrooms
sundried tomatoes

Bring the water, salt, pepper and thyme to a boil in a large saucepan. Slowly beat in the polenta with a whisk to avoid lumps. Reduce the heat to low and stir to prevent sticking. Cook slowly for 10 minutes.

In a separate pan, saute the mushrooms and green onions in 2 tablespoons of butter till cooked through and just beginning to brown. Season with a little salt and pepper, add the wine and reduce until most of the wine cooks away. Add to the polenta mixture with the remaining butter and parsley.

Off the heat, spread the polenta mixture on a butter cake pan or cookie sheet so that it's approximately 1/2 inch thick. Cool, cover with plastic and refrigerate up to a day in advance.

To complete the dish, cut the polenta into diamonds or other interesting shapes. Grill over mesquite until the surface is lightly toasted. (Grill some fresh shiitake mushrooms as well - careful not to burn - set aside for garnish). Turn, place a slice of fontina cheese on top and allow it to just melt. Serve warm garnished with grilled shiitake mushrooms and slivers of sun-dried tomatoes.

Serves 6-8.

Summer

Grande Potatoes

Georgia Peter, Grower

4 or 5 potatoes (Russet or red)
1/3 cup of butter or margarine
1/2 of an onion, coarsely chopped
1/2 of a red bell pepper, coarsely chopped
1   10 1/2-ounce can of cream of celery
   soup
1/2 cup of milk
4 ounces of cheddar cheese, grated
2 drops of hot pepper sauce
1   4-ounce can of chopped green chillies,
   drained
1/2 teaspoon of salt
1/4   cup of cheddar cheese, grated

Boil the potatoes with their skins on until done.
Drain them, let them cool, then thinly slice them.

Preheat your oven to 350°F. In a skillet, melt the
butter and saute the onions and peppers until tender. Add the soup and milk and 4 ounces of cheese.
Cook over a low heat, stirring, until the cheese
melts. Stir in the hot pepper sauce, green chillies
and salt. Add the sliced potatoes and stir.

Pour into a greased casserole and top with the 1/4
cup of grated cheese. Bake for 30 minutes or until
nice and bubbly.

Serves 6-8.

summer

Grande Potatoes

Georgia Peter, Grower

2 medium eggplant
2 eggs
1 pint of milk
2 cups of bread crumbs
1 teaspoon of salt
1 teaspoon of pepper
1 cup of flour
1 8-ounce package of cream cheese
12 ounces of spinach, chopped
8 artichoke hearts (in juice)
8-10 slices of swiss cheese (1/8 inch thick)
Bearnaise Sauce (see page 58)

Preheat your oven to 340°F.

Peel and slice the eggplant 1/2 inch thick. Mix the eggs and milk together and whip. Season the bread crumbs with the salt and pepper. Lightly bread the eggplant by dipping first in flour, then the egg mixture, then bread crumbs.

Place the eggplant slices on an oiled or buttered sheet pan and bake for 7-10 minutes. Remove from the oven and set aside.

Mix the cream cheese and spinach together. After the eggplant has cooled, top each eggplant slice with a small scoop of the cream cheese/spinach mixture, then an artichoke heart, then a slice of swiss cheese.   Rebake at 350°F. for 7-10 minutes. Serve with Bearnaise Sauce.

Serves 4.

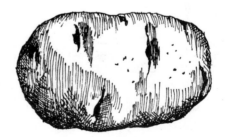

summer

57

Eggplant Florentine

Chef Pierre, Chez Peyo

2 medium eggplant
2 eggs
1 pint of milk
2 cups of bread crumbs
1 teaspoon of salt
1 teaspoon of pepper
1 cup of flour
1 8-ounce package of cream cheese
12 ounces of spinach, chopped
8 artichoke hearts (in juice)
8-10 slices of swiss cheese (1/8 inch thick)
Bearnaise Sauce (see page 58)

Preheat your oven to 340°F.

Peel and slice the eggplant 1/2 inch thick. Mix the eggs and milk together and whip. Season the bread crumbs with the salt and pepper. Lightly bread the eggplant by dipping first in flour, then the egg mixture, then bread crumbs.

Place the eggplant slices on an oiled or buttered sheet pan and bake for 7-10 minutes. Remove from the oven and set aside.

Mix the cream cheese and spinach together. After the eggplant has cooled, top each eggplant slice with a small scoop of the cream cheese/spinach mixture, then an artichoke heart, then a slice of swiss cheese. Rebake at 350°F. for 7-10 minutes. Serve with Bearnaise Sauce.

Serves 4.

European botanists once thought that eating eggplant caused insanity, hence it was nicknamed "Mad Apple". Aside from the common purple ones, eggplant can also come in green, white, orange, and even striped colors.

Summer

Bearnaise Sauce

Chef Pierre, Chez Peyo

2 cloves of shallots
1/4 teaspoon of tarragon, chopped
1/2 cup of red wine vinegar
1 1/2 cups of butter
4 egg yolks
1/8 cup of water
1 teaspoon of lemon juice
1 teaspoon of salt
2 tablespoons of chopped parsley

Dice the shallots very finely. In a small saucepan, mix the diced shallots with tarragon and red wine vinegar. Cook over a medium flame until all of the liquid evaporates. Set aside to cool. Melt the butter (but do not boil it). It must be warm.

Put the egg yolks in a small stainless steel bowl with the water and lemon juice and whip. Place over a low flame, constantly whipping until the mixture is fluffy and smooth or until the bubbles disappear. DO NOT SCRAMBLE THE EGGS. They should be smooth and creamy. Remove from the flame and slowly add the warm melted butter, a little at a time, until gone, whipping constantly. Add the tarragon mixture and salt and parsley to taste.

Yields 4 servings.

Serve with Eggplant Florentine, page 58 or Lamb Wellington, page 14.

summer

Raspberry Bread

Roancy Aubin, Sonoma Berry Patch

This recipe is best if mixed by hand instead of with a mixer. If frozen raspberries are used, do not thaw completely but use individually frozen berries. Fresh raspberries crush very easily so they must be folded into the batter very carefully so as to retain their shape.

3/4 cup of butter
3/4 cup of sugar
3 eggs
2 cups of flour
2 teaspoons of baking powder
1 teaspoon of baking soda
1/2 teaspoon of salt
1 cup of sour milk (or buttermilk)
1 teaspoon of vanilla
1 1/2 cups of fresh (or frozen) raspberries
1 cup of chopped pecans or walnuts (optional)

Preheat the oven to 350°F. Cream the butter and sugar together. Add the eggs, beating well. In another bowl, mix the other dry ingredients, then add them alternately with sour milk to the egg mixture. Add the vanilla. Gently fold in the nuts and raspberries. Pour the batter into two 4" x 8" x 2" loaf pans and bake for 45-55 minutes.

Makes two loaves.

You can make this bread in the raspberry off-season by getting fresh berries in season and flash-freezing them on a cookie sheet, then transferring them to well-sealed plastic bags.

Zucchini Bread

Bob and Jo Kearns, Growers

Try this bread warm and spread with butter, jam or cream cheese.

2 eggs
1 cup of oil
2 teaspoons of vanilla
2 cups of sugar
3 cups of flour
1 teaspoon of baking soda
1 teaspoon of cinnamon
1/4 teaspoon of baking powder
1 teaspoon of salt
3 cups of grated zucchini
1/2 cup of nuts (optional)
1/4 teaspoon of nutmeg (optional)
1/2 cup of raisins (optional)

Preheat oven to 350°F.

Mix the eggs, oil and vanilla together, then add the sugar, flour, soda, cinnamon, baking powder and salt. Mix well and add the zucchini, nuts, nutmeg and raisins.

Pour the batter into 2 greased loaf pans and bake for one hour.

Makes two hot delicious loaves.

If you can find them, try zucchini or squash blossoms some time. Stuff them with a soft, tangy cheese, then batter and fry them.

summer

Raspberry-Tarte Squares

Bob Schreck, Chalais of Oakmont

LINZER CRUST:

all-purpose flour
sugar
finely ground almonds
butter
cinnamon

Mix equal parts of flour, sugar, almonds and butter, say, one cup of each. Flavor with cinnamon and mix it into a cookie dough. Let it rest a bit, then roll it over an upside down jelly roll pan or 1/2 sheet cake pan. Bake it at 220°F. until golden brown.

1 quart of currant jelly
sponge cake
a pound or more of fresh raspberries
sliced roasted almonds

While the crust is baking, bring the quart of currant jelly to a boil. When the crust is ready, brush and seal it with currant jelly. Top it with a layer of 1/8"

sponge cake and brush and seal with currant jelly again.

Layer this base with fresh raspberries as tight as possible and glaze with hot currant jelly. Finish borders with roasted sliced almonds. Let the tart set up and then slice it into any sized pieces you want.

Summer

62

Mellow Melon

Elizabeth Gregson

1 large watermelon
1/2 of a cantaloupe, scooped in balls
white grapes
red grapes
3 or 4 bananas, sliced
5 or 6 peeled and separated oranges
pineapple chunks
1 lemon, sliced
1 lime, sliced
2 or 3 apples, sliced
3 kiwis, sliced
2 bottles of your favorite white or rose wine
2 bottles of Sprite or Slice soda

Slice a section of the watermelon off, without cutting into the pink part, to make a flat spot for it to stand on. Sit it flat and cut a section out of the top, then scoop out the center in balls. Mix it with the other fruit and put it all into the hollowed watermelon with the wine.

Serve in glasses with Sprite or Slice soda, or over ice cream.

You can also reduce the amount of wine, and it's great over pound cake. No refrigeration needed.

This is a great thing to put together for a summer party.

summer

63

Peach Crisp

Phillips Farm

You can peel the peaches for this recipe if you like.

1 cup of flour
1 cup of light brown sugar
grated rind of one lemon
1/2 cup of cold butter
4 cups of fresh sliced peaches
the juice of one lemon

Preheat the oven to 375°F.

Mix the flour, sugar, lemon rind and butter together well until it resembles coarse meal. Put the peaches in a greased shallow baking dish and sprinkle with lemon juice. Press the crumb mixture on top. Bake for 25 minutes, or until nicely golden.

Try it warm over or under ice cream, or alone sprinkled with crushed roasted almonds.

A fresh-picked, juicy peach, one that's not too tart, not too dry or bland, is one of the best things life has to offer. Be selective! Don't settle for those softball-sized, rock-hard peaches that the clerk assures you will "soften and sweeten up at home." Once they're off the tree, they'll never get any sweeter.

Pears in Red Wine

Chef Josef Keller, La Province Restaurant

5 pears
1 quart of burgundy
1 cup of sugar
1 tablespoon of honey
1/2 teaspoon of cinnamon
juice of 1/2 of a lemon
1/8 teaspoon of vanilla extract
1 clove
1 teaspoon of cornstarch
a dash of Triple Sec
vanilla ice cream
toasted almonds

Peel, core, and halve, quarter or slice the pears; combine the next seven ingredients in a large pan and add the pears. Simmer for 30 minutes or until the fruit is soft; remove the pears from the liquid and set them aside.

To the liquid, add the cornstarch dissolved in a dash of Triple Sec; bring to a quick boil, then remove from the heat. Add the pears back to the liquid and cool.

Let this sit for a day or two to develop it's full flavor. Serve it warm or cold over good vanilla ice cream and sprinkle with toasted almonds.

Serves 10.

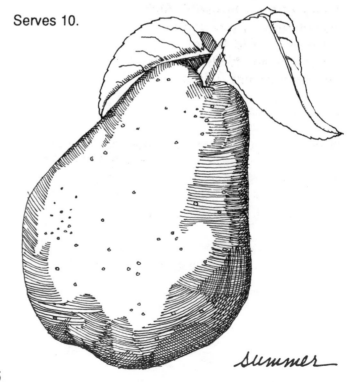

Summer

65

Watermelon Sherbet

Jill Brown

This is hard to beat as a refreshing, delicious summer dessert.

3 cups of pureed watermelon (without seeds!)
1/4 cup of sugar
1/4 teaspoon of salt
1/2 cup of light corn syrup
1/4 cup of lemon juice

Puree the melon in a blender if possible. Add the remaining ingredients to the watermelon and stir until the sugar is dissolved. Turn the mixture into freezer trays and freeze until just firm. Put it all into a bowl and beat until it's light and fluffy, then return it to the freezer until it reaches sherbet consistency.

" The Farmers Market is human, with real people and real food!
– Barbara Bray

summer

Sour Apricot and Raspberry Buckle

Lisa Hemenway, Hemenway Restaurant

I grew up next to apricot orchards and worked summers in the orchards. To this day I remember the taste of a great apricot. They've never seemed to taste as good, and it seems they are usually too sour. Here's a recipe for sour apricots!

2 pounds of fruit -- a mixture of sliced apricots and raspberries tossed with 3/4 of a cup of sugar and set aside (more apricots than raspberries)

1 cube (4 ounces) of sweet butter
3/4 cup of sugar
2 cups of flour
1/2 teaspoon of salt
2 teaspoons of baking powder
2/3 cup of milk
2 eggs

ALMOND STREUSEL TOPPING:

2/3 cup of sugar
1/3 cup of flour
1/3 cup of ground almonds
1/2 cup of butter, cut into bits

Preheat the oven to 350°F.

Cream the butter with the 3/4 cup of sugar. Sift together the flour, salt and baking powder and add to the butter mixture. Add the milk and eggs and mix until incorporated. Fold in 1 cup of the fruit mixture and press this into the bottom of a 9" square pan.

Pour the remaining fruit mixture over. Mix up the Streusel Topping until it's nice and crumbly (using the paddle of your mixer if you have one). Sprinkle this over the fruit and bake for approximately an hour.

Summer

67

FALL

"I remember the autumns of my childhood with nostalgia. Picking prunes, cutting grapes, hulling walnuts, and picking corn, tomatoes, pears -- every farm kitchen diligently prepared for winter. Outside, the smell of drying prunes, peaches and pears permeated the air. For me, the harvest time activities are the most exciting of all of the seasons. The farmer finally reaps his reward from labor and patience."

- Dana McIntosh

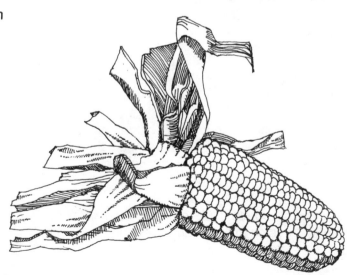

Cabbage Borsht

Helen Shainsky, Acalde for Sonoma

Helen is the honorary mayor of Sonoma, and an expert in Jewish cookery.

2 pounds of soup meat (your choice)
a soup bone
1 onion, chopped
2 cups of fresh tomatoes, chopped
6 cups of cold water
salt and pepper to taste
1 head of cabbage
1 cup of julienned beets
1/2 cup of raisins
sugar to taste
lemon juice to taste

Add the soup meat, soup bone, onion, and tomatoes to the water in a large kettle. Add salt and pepper to taste. Cover, bring everything to a boil and simmer slowly for 2-3 hours.

Wash and shred the cabbage. Add the cabbage, beets and raisins to the soup, and cook for 30 minutes or until the meat is tender. Add sugar and lemon juice to taste and simmer 30 minutes more.

Serves 6.

fall

70

Cauliflower Soup

Chef Josef Keller, La Province Restaurant

2 medium heads of fresh cauliflower
1/4 of a leek
2 stalks of celery
1 medium onion
1 medium potato
2 ounces of butter
1/2 cup of uncooked rice
1 quart of chicken broth
1 pint of cream
2 cups of milk
Worcestershire sauce, soy sauce, salt and
   pepper to taste

Separate the flowers from the cauliflower head.
Chop all of the other vegetables, including the remainder of the cauliflower, into bite-sized chunks.
Saute the vegetables in hot melted butter for 3 minutes, stirring constantly. Add the rice and chicken
broth and simmer uncovered for 30 to 45 minutes
(rice and vegetables should be tender).

Puree everything in a blender or food processor.
Add the cream, milk and seasoning. Add a small
amount of chicken base or bouillon if more flavor is
desired. Simmer for 10 to 15 more minutes, and
serve hot.

Serves 10 to 12.

Even cauliflower-haters will love this soup.

fall

French Onion Soup

Patricia Shaw

Sauteeing the onions in this recipe slowly brings out their full rich flavor.

3 pounds of onions, chopped
3/4 of a cube of butter
8 cups of stock, or 8 cups of water plus 10
  bouillon cubes
1/2 cup of wine
1 cup of shredded swiss cheese

Heat up a heavy 5 quart pot; melt the butter in it. Add the onions and saute them slowly until they're golden brown and the juices have carmelized on the bottom of the pan (this can take an hour or more).

Add the stock or bouillon & water; bring to a boil, scraping the bottom of the pan several times to incorporate the carmelized onion juices into the broth.

Put the lid on the pot and simmer the soup gently for one hour or more! (The longer the broth and onions simmer -- the more patient you are -- the better the flavor).

Fifteen minutes before serving, add the wine and bring back to a simmer.

To serve, place 2-3 tablespoons of swiss cheese in the bottom of each bowl. Ladle the onion soup over the cheese. Serve hot with french bread or garlic bread. Enjoy!!

Serves 8-10.

fall

Sweet Red Bell Pepper Soup

Chef John Ash, John Ash & Co.

6 cups of chopped yellow onions
6 cups of seeded and chopped red bell
  pepper
2 cloves of garlic, chopped
1/4 cup of butter
2 cups of ripe tomatoes, peeled & seeded
2 quarts of good chicken or mushroom
  stock
2 tablespoons of sweet paprika
1/2 teaspoon EACH of whole thyme and oregano
1/3 cup of brandy
heavy cream
salt and pepper

edible flower petals (optional) for garnish

Saute the onions, peppers and garlic in butter until soft. Add the tomatoes, stock, paprika and herbs; simmer 15-20 minutes. Add the brandy and correct the seasoning to your taste; simmer 5 minutes more.

Puree the soup in a food processor or blender. Return it to the pan and reheat. Add the cream, correct the seasoning again and serve immediately.

Garnish the soup with flower petals such as calendula or sweetheart roses.

Serves 10-12.

All sweet bell peppers are green when immature, and become red, yellow, orange or purple when they ripen. They're a great source of vitamin C -- better than lemons, limes or oranges.

fall

Fruit Salad

Ethel Mannis

1 small can of pineapple chunks
2 apples, chopped
3 bananas, sliced
1 can of fruit cocktail
1 small can of mandarin oranges, drained
1/2 cup of chopped walnuts
any other fruit you love to eat

DRESSING:

1/2 cup of sugar
2 tablespoons of flour
1/2 cup of milk
2 tablespoons of vinegar
1 tablespoon of vanilla

Mix all of the fruit together and set it aside (in the fridge if you like it cold). Mix all of the dressing ingredients except the vanilla; cook over medium heat, stirring, until thickened. Add the vanilla. Cool and fold it into the fruit mixture.

Serves 6-8.

fall

Cabbage -Apple Slaw

Marie Schutz

Mix together:
6 cups of shredded fresh cabbage
1/2 cup of chopped walnuts
1 cup of chopped tart unpeeled apples
3/4 teaspoon of salt
3/4 teaspoon of ginger

Toss with a dressing of:
1/2 cup of mayonnaise
1 tablespoon of apple cider vinegar
1 tablespoon of honey

Garnish with:
Parsley and paprika

Serves 6-8.

Jambalaya

Keith Bladen

This recipe is based on a traditional Louisiana recipe. It's colorful, hearty and delicious, and is best served with tall bottles of icy cold beer.

1 chicken, cut up
3/4 pound of andouille sausage, diced
1 red onion, diced
1 cup of diced green onions
1 medium red bell pepper
1 medium yellow bell pepper
1/4 cup of salad oil
4 cloves of garlic
3 cups of short grain rice
5 cups of chicken broth
1/2 teaspoon of cayenne pepper
1/2 tablespoon of paprika
1/2 cup of chopped parsley
salt and pepper to taste
1 1/2 cups of chopped celery

Heat the oil in a large kettle. Saute the sausage until slightly browned; remove and reserve. Salt and pepper the chicken pieces and fry them in the oil until browned; remove and reserve. Saute the vegies and garlic in the oil until tender (just for a couple of minutes if you want to see them in the dish). Add back the sausage and chicken; mix in the cayenne, paprika and parsley. Add the broth, stir and bring to a boil. Reduce the heat to a simmer, add the rice and cook for 25 minutes or until the rice is cooked and all of the liquid is absorbed.

Andouille sausage is a great spicy Cajun sausage which can (thankfully) be found in better-than-average groceries and sausage shops.

fall

Mesquite Grilled Veal Loin

Chef Todd Muir, Madrona Manor

To make the marinade, mix well:
1/2 cup white wine
juice of one lemon and its diced flesh
1 tablespoon of coriander seeds, crushed
4 springs of fresh thyme
4 sprigs of parsley
white pepper, cracked, to taste
then pour it over
4 veal loin steaks, 5 ounces each
and marinate them for 4 hours.

CORN AND RED PEPPER SALSA:
4 roasted red peppers, blackened, skinned
  and pureed
corn kernels from one ear of corn, blanched
1/2 cup of olive oil
juice from one lemon
1 tablespoon of cilantro, chopped coarsely
  (optional)
salt and pepper to taste

BABY VEGETABLE RAGOUT
16 cloves of whole roast garlic, peeled

12 baby carrots, cooked
12 baby yellow squash, cooked
12 baby turnips, cooked
12 creamer or boiling onions, cooked and
  peeled
butter to saute
1/2 cup of reduced veal stock
1 cup of cream, reduced by 1/2
1/4 cup of Mexican black beans, cooked
1 teaspoon of cumin
2 teaspoons of oregano
salt and pepper to taste
cilantro for garnish (optional)

Mix the salsa ingredients and set aside. Saute the vegetables in butter and add the reduced stock and cream to desired thickness (sauce should nap the back of a spoon). Add the beans and spices and season to taste.

Grill or saute the veal loin medium rare. Place some sauce on the plate, center the veal and dollop with salsa. Serves 4-6.

fall

76

Fiesta Sonoma Grilled Turkey

Rich and Saralee Kunde

1/2 cup of cilantro
1/2 cup of lime juice
1/2 cup of Sonoma County Sauvignon
   Blanc wine
1/2 cup of olive oil
4 garlic cloves, crushed
6 turkey tenderloins (fillets) 6-8 oz. each
salt & pepper to taste
fresh lime slices   (optional)

Clean the cilantro, remove the leaves and add them to the lime juice, wine, olive oil, and crushed garlic to form the marinade.

Pour the marinade over the turkey, cover tightly and refrigerate for several hours, preferably overnight.

Season the turkey with salt and pepper and grill 6 inches above medium hot coals for 8 minutes on each side. Brush with marinade several times during grilling for a beautiful golden color.

Serve with a squeeze of fresh lime for added flavor.

Wine suggestions: Sonoma County Sauvignon Blanc or Fume Blanc is a logical choice, but turkey complements so many wines from white to blush to red that your favorite wine is without question the best one to serve with this meal.

Serves 6.

Cilantro (the seeds of the same plant are known as coriander) is the pungent herb responsible for making Mexican food taste like Mexican food. Halfway around the world, it is also commonly used in Chinese cookery.

fall

Chicken Sebastopol

Chef Kirby Tubb, Plaza Grill

4 8-ounce chicken breasts, whole, boned
   and skinned
6 ounces of brie, thinly sliced
1 medium Gravenstein (or other tart) apple

SAUCE:

1 ounce of clarified butter or oil
1 tablespoon of shallots, finely minced
2 medium Gravenstein apples, peeled and
   julienned
1/2 cup of Calvados or Brandy
2 cups of heavy whipping cream

Pound the chicken breasts. Place 1 1/2 ounces of thinly sliced brie and 6-8 apple slices inside of each chicken breast. Roll them up and fold the ends in. Chill for 2-4 hours. Grill them over a mesquite or charcoal BBQ until done.

Make the sauce just before serving: Saute the shallots and apples in the hot butter until slightly cooked but not brown. Add the Calvados and flame. Add the cream and cook over medium high heat until reduced by one third and the sauce is thick and creamy. Place 1/4 of the sauce on each plate. Slice chicken breasts across diagonally into 4-5 pieces and fan out onto each plate on top of the sauce. Serve immediately.

Serves 4.

fall

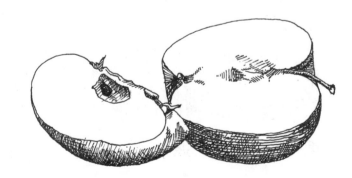

Pumpkin Ravioli with Brie Nutmeg Cream

Lisa Hemenway

Wendy Porter

Asiago cheese for this recipe can be found in Italian delicatessens.

a 3-pound raw pumpkin
2 leeks, chopped finely
2 stalks of celery, chopped finely
8 tablespoons of butter
nutmeg to taste
1 cup of asiago cheese
salt and pepper to taste
bread crumbs (for the right consistency)
sheet ravioli pasta

Bake the pumpkin with a little butter and nutmeg until tender.

Saute the chopped leeks and celery in 8 tablespoons of butter for several minutes. Scoop out the pumpkin and add it to the saute mixture. Spice with nutmeg, salt and pepper to taste. Add 1 cup of asiago cheese.

Put everything in a food processor or blender and puree (not too fine). Fold in enough bread crumbs for the filling to stay where you want it, fill your raviolis and cook them in slightly salted boiling water until the pasta is done. Serve with Brie Nutmeg Cream Sauce (recipe follows).

BRIE NUTMEG CREAM

1/2 pound of brie (not too ripe)
1/2 pound of sweet butter
1/2 cup of asiago cheese
5 egg yolks
2 cups of half-and-half
1 tablespoon of nutmeg

Soften the brie and butter; mix until combined. Add the asiago. While mixing add the egg yolks one at a time until incorporated. Fold in the half-and-half and nutmeg. Heat all in a saucepan, stirring constantly. This is like making a custard sauce -- heat and stir just until the eggs are thickened. Don't overcook or it will curdle. Serve over Pumpkin Raviolis.

fall

Potato Pancakes

Helen Shainsky, Acalde for Sonoma

It's best to hide these while you're cooking them if you have people wandering through your kitchen. They won't last long.

6 **medium potatoes**
1 **small onion**
2 **extra large or 3 large eggs**
1/2 **cup of matzo meal**
1/2 **teaspoon of baking powder**
salt **and pepper to taste**

Peel and grate the potatoes and onion. Let them stand for 10 minutes so that their liquid will rise to the top. Remove and discard the liquid. Mix the potatoes and onion together; stir in the eggs, matzo meal, baking powder, salt and pepper.

Drop the batter by the spoonful onto a hot, well-greased griddle (I use corn oil). Brown them on both sides, then drain on absorbent paper.

Serve hot with applesauce, sugar or sour cream.

fall

Here are some potato equivalents: One pound of potatoes = about 3 medium potatoes = 3 cups peeled and sliced = 2½ cups peeled and diced = 2 cups of mashed or french-fried potatoes. Whew.

Stuffed Cabbage Rolls

Dianne Hoskins, Hoskins Ranch

1 large white onion, chopped
1 pound of ground beef
1 large cabbage (10 large leaves are
   needed)
4 cups of cooked rice
a pint of tomato sauce plus 1/2 pint for simmering (try ours! page 147)

Saute the onion and ground beef until the onion is tender and the beef cooked through. Mix in the rice and pint of tomato sauce. Set aside.

Cut the cabbage leaves at the base of the head and peel off carefully. Drop them in boiling water and cook until tender. Cool them off immediately in cool water and place them flat on a working surface.

Take a spoonful of the rice mixture and place it in the center of each leaf. Fold the leaves over the mixture and roll up. Place all in a skillet and simmer with 1/2 pint of tomato sauce over the top of them. Sprinkle cheese over everything if desired.

Simmer for 30 minutes. Season as desired.

Serves 4-6.

Hoskins Ranch in Healdsburg has been in Dianne's family for 80 years. There are now four generations on the ranch.

fall

81

Beans for Autumn Meatless Chili

Hilda Swartz, Manager of the Farmers Markets

1/2 of a large onion, chopped
1 clove of garlic, chopped
1/4 cup of chopped green peppers
2 tablespoons of corn or olive oil
2 medium tomatoes, peeled and sliced
1/2 cup of chopped cabbage
1 can of red kidney beans

Simmer the onion, garlic and green peppers in 2 tablespoons of corn or olive oil in a large skillet. Add the peeled and sliced tomatoes, chopped cabbage and beans (with their liquid).

Simmer covered for 30 minutes. Serve with crackers or whole wheat bread.

Serves 2.

To the "Beans for Autumn" recipe, simply delete the cabbage and add 1 can of tomato soup plus1 teaspoon of Mexican blend spice.

Serve with grated cheese and corn chips.

These are quick and tasty dishes, high in protein and nutrients.

fall

Quick Harvest Dinner

Richard Hambright, Grower

Richard says of his oyster mushrooms: "Please don't wash these beautiful mushrooms. No soil or manure is used to grow them! Don't overcook these exotic mushrooms. They cook very quickly and can always be added as the last ingredient. They're also good raw!"

1 cup of cooked wild rice
1/4 pound of fresh oyster mushrooms
2 small zucchini, sliced into bite-sized
   pieces
1 medium tomato or 1/2 cup of cherry toma-
   toes, sliced
1/4 pound of your favorite cheese, grated
chervil for seasoning

Preheat the oven to 350°F. Layer the rice in the bottom of an ovenproof or microwave safe dish. Arrange in layers from bottom to top: zucchini slices, oyster mushrooms, then tomato. Layer the cheese over all and sprinkle with chervil. Cover and heat in conventional oven for about 20 minutes at 350°F., or in a microwave, heat on high for 3 minutes.

We suggest serving this dish with a crisp green salad made from red leaf lettuce, green bell peppers, snow peas, jicama and alfalfa sprouts, with a sweet mustard dressing.

A dessert of fresh fruit tops off this harvest dinner perfectly.

Serves 4-6.

fall

Eggplant Parmesan

Ursula Crane

1 medium eggplant
2 cups of fine bread crumbs
safflower or olive oil for frying

SAUCE:

6 fresh tomatoes
1 onion, finely chopped
3 celery stalks, chopped
1/2 cup of parsley
1/2 cup of cilantro
1/2 teaspoon of oregano
4 garlic cloves, chopped
salt and pepper to taste

2 cups of Parmesan cheese
large chunks of tofu

Wash the eggplant under warm water with a brush. Slice it 1/2 " thick, cutting off the ends. Put it into a colander, rubbing both sides with salt. Let it stand for an hour, then wash it with cold water and pat dry with a towel. Put the slices on a platter and sprinkle fine bread crumbs on both sides. Let stand for 1/2 hour. Fry them in a heavy skillet with safflower oil or olive oil until golden.and tender.

Mix up the sauce ingredients and simmer for 15 minutes. Add salt, pepper, and additional spices to taste.

Preheat the oven to 350°F. Spoon some of the simmered sauce in the bottom of an oiled casserole.

Add the eggplant, Parmesan, tofu and sauce in layers until everything is used up. Cover and bake for 1 hour.

Serves 6.

fall

Perfect Potatoes

Georgia Peter, Grower

1 cup of hot water
1 packet of dry onion soup mix
1/2 cup of butter, melted
1/4 teaspoon each of pepper and salt
8 medium or small potatoes, unpeeled, cut
   into 1" cubes
a sprinkling of fresh chopped parsley

Preheat your oven to 350°F.

Combine the water, soup mix, butter, salt and pepper in a 2-quart casserole. Add the potatoes and stir. Bake for 1 1/2 hours. Sprinkle with parsley before serving.

Serves 6-8.

There are lots of different kinds of potatoes grown these days... in addition to the standard reds, whites and Russets, try Yukon Golds, Yellow Finns, and the fabulous Royal Purples. Startle your kids with a batch of purple mashed potatoes!!

fall

Sweet and Sour Cabbage

Arnold Kochman

1/6 of a stick of butter
1/8 cup of white flour
a handful of black currants
1/2 of a red cabbage, coarsely shredded
2 tablespoons of cilantro, finely chopped
1/2 teaspoon of salt
1/8 cup of vinegar
1/8 cup of brown sugar

Melt the butter; add the flour and cook, stirring constantly until slightly brown. Add a little water and stir until smooth. Add the black currants. Add the cabbage and cilantro and enough water to cook. Simmer, stirring occasionally until the cabbage is soft. Add the salt, vinegar and sugar and simmer some more until the liquid thickens into a sauce. Adjust the vinegar and sugar to taste, and serve.

fall

Baked Green Peppers with Feta, Tomato and Walnuts

Mary Ann Nardo

"This recipe involves roasting the peppers before stuffing and baking them. I think this really brings out the flavor more than just steaming or baking them. I like to use sheep feta, available at health food stores, rather than regular feta. It's milder and not as salty.

4 large green peppers, roasted
1/2 - 3/4 cup of crumbled feta cheese
1 egg
1 1/2 cups of cooked brown or white rice
1/4 cup of walnuts
1/2 cup of tomatoes
1/4 teaspoon of marjoram

Roast the peppers under a broiler until blacked all over (turning if necessary). Cool them in a paper sack and peel their skins off. The peppers will be soft and collapsed.

Preheat your oven to 350° F. Remove as much juice from the tomatoes as possible and chop. Mix them well with the rest of the ingredients, slit the peppers and stuff the mixture inside. Lay them on a cookie sheet or in a cake pan - GENTLY, they'll be fragile. Drizzle olive oil over the top if you desire and bake them for a half-hour or until the egg is cooked through.

Serves 4.

fall

Two Broads Knock-Your-Socks-Off Salsa

Kim Morgan and Marge Terrian

This salsa, we think, is about as good as life gets.

4 medium tomatoes, diced
1/2 medium onion, diced
1/4 bell pepper, red or yellow, diced
2 cloves of garlic, diced
1 tablespoon of fresh cilantro, minced
4 ounce can of green chiles, diced
2 to 6 slices of (canned) pickled Jalapeno
   peppers, diced
1 cup (or half of a 15-ounce can) tomato
   sauce
1 tablespoon of vinegar

1 tablespoon of sugar
1 teaspoon of chili powder
1/2 teaspoon of salt
1/4 teaspoon of cumin

Mix everything together well. Cook, uncovered, for 5 minutes. Chill before serving. It's great with chips, Mexican dishes, omelettes, or as a flavoring ingredient for any dish that needs a kick. Yields 4 cups.

fall

Now, we make this salsa using Kim's brother-in-law's pickled Jalapeño peppers, but it's not the end of the world if you can't find Bill or don't have a pepper-growing brother-in-law. Just use canned, pickled Jalapeño slices ... 2 if you're lightweight, 6 or more if you have an asbestos mouth.

Italian Marinara Sauce

Congressman Doug Bosco

7 cups of homemade tomato sauce or 2
    28-oz. cans of store-bought (try ours!
    page 147)
3/4 cup of good olive oil
4 cloves of garlic (or as much as you like)
1 teaspoon of salt
pepper to taste
2 teaspoons of sugar
2 tablespoons of fresh basil
dash of red pepper if you like

In a sauce pan, fry the garlic until golden brown --
don't burn it -- then add the rest of the ingredients to
the pan. Bring to a boil. Simmer for 1 hour or more,
stirring occasionally so it doesn't stick. The longer
you cook it the thicker it gets. Delicious over pasta,
vegetables, meats.

Serves 4.

Fast Spaghetti Sauce

Pete Petersen, Grower

2 medium onions
2 cans or 1 1/2 quarts of tomato sauce
    (try ours! page 147)
1/4 teaspoon of sage
1/4 teaspoon of rosemary
1/4 teaspoon of oregano
4 cloves of garlic, chopped
1 or 2 cups of chicken broth

Chop the onion or run it through a food processor.
Saute it in a little oil until it's almost brown. Add the
tomato sauce, spices, and chopped garlic and simmer for 20 minutes. Add the broth (one or two cups,
depending on how thick you like your sauce!) and
simmer for 25 minutes longer.

Serves 6.

Pete Peterson is a Danish grower who raises terrific pumpkins.

89

fall

Sauce for Leftover Meats

Doris Lester

1/4 cup of butter or margarine
1/2 cup of bread crumbs (for thickening)
2 cups of chicken broth (homemade or
    made with bouillon cubes)
1/2 teaspoon of thyme
10 cloves of garlic (chopped)
salt and pepper to taste
leftover meats

Mix all of the ingredients and simmer for 2 hours in a double boiler, stirring occasionally. Cut your leftover lamb, beef, chicken or veal into bite-sized pieces and stir them into the sauce. Heat everything just long enough to heat through. Serve over boiled beans, rice, or pasta.

Spicy Kiwi Meat Sauce

Mooney Farms

Use this delicious sweet and sour sauce on poultry, fish or ribs.

4 tablespoons of Mooney Farms Kiwi, Kiwi
    Orange or Kiwi Pineapple jam
1/4 teaspoon of lemon juice
1/4 cup of water
2 cloves of garlic, minced
1/4 onion, grated
1/2 teaspoon of dry mustard
1 teaspoon of Worcestershire sauce
salt and pepper to taste

Mix all of the ingredients together in a saucepan. Heat to a boil, stirring, and simmer for 3 minutes.

Brush the sauce onto your meat 10 minutes before it's done.

fall

Pumpkin Bread
Laurie Anderson

2 cups of white sugar
1 cup of brown sugar
1 cup of oil
4 eggs
3-1/2 cups of flour
2 cups of pumpkin, grated
1 1/2 teaspoon of salt
2 teaspoons of baking soda
1 teaspoon of cinnamon
1 teaspoon of nutmeg
3/4 cup of water
1/2 cup of walnuts

Preheat the oven to 350°F. Mix everything together well in a large mixing bowl. Bake in two well-greased loaf pans for 45 minutes to an hour, or until golden brown and a toothpick inserted in the middle comes out clean.

Makes two hot, fragrant loaves.

Apple Bread
Flora Early, Grower

2 cups of flour
1/2 cup of sugar
1 cup of applesauce (preferably homemade)
1 teaspoon of vanilla
a pinch of salt
2 eggs
2/3 cup of oil
1 teaspoon of baking soda
2 teaspoons of baking powder
1-1/2 teaspoons of cinnamon

Preheat your oven to 350°F. Mix all of the ingredients well and bake in a loaf pan for approximately 35 to 40 minutes. Easy and delicious!

Yields one loaf.

"It's easy for apples to be bruised-- handle carefully and don't abuse."

fall

Scones

Flora Early, Grower

1 cube (4 oz.) of butter
1 egg
3 cups of flour
3 teaspoons of baking powder
1 teaspoon of baking soda
a pinch of salt
1/2 cup of sugar
the grated rind of 1 lemon
the juice of that same lemon
1 cup of buttermilk
1 1/2 cups of raisins or currants

Melt the butter. Cool it a bit, then mix in the egg. Add the flour, baking powder, soda, and salt and mix well. Add the lemon rind and juice, then the buttermilk and raisins or currants. Working with your hands and adding more flour if necessary, shape the dough into large biscuits. Moisten each with a bit of sweet milk to help them brown, then sprinkle with cinnamon sugar.

Bake them on greased cookie sheets at 350° F. for approximately 20 to 25 minutes.

Ask the growers at the Santa Rosa Farmers Markets about Flora's scones and watch their eyes glaze over. These little beauties can be eaten "plain" or slathered with butter or jam.

fall

Kiwi Freezer Ice Cream

Helen Crowder, Grower

2 1/2 cups of mashed kiwifruit
1/2 cup of sugar
2 quarts of half and half
1 pint of milk
4 eggs
1/2 cup of sweetened condensed milk
1 cup more of sugar
1/4 teaspoon of salt
green food coloring

Peel & mash the kiwifruit and cook it with a half cup of sugar for 5 minutes, bringing the mixture to boil and then reducing the temperature to a simmer. Set aside.

Heat 2 cups of the half and half with all of the milk in the top of a double boiler to boil, then reduce the heat to about medium to keep the water at a low boil or simmer. The water should not touch the bottom of the section with half and half, or the half and half will scorch.

Beat the eggs slightly. Add the condensed milk, cup of sugar and salt to them. Into the egg mixture, blend a little of the hot cream, then slowly add this to the mixture in the double boiler (this prevents the eggs from curdling when added to the hot liquid). Cook 5 minutes, stirring, to 176 degrees Fahrenheit or until the mixture will coat a spoon. Cool.

Stir in the remaining half and half and kiwifruit, along with a few drops of green food coloring if you'd like it to be greener.

Freeze in an ice-and-coarse-salt mixture or in a standard ice cream freezer.

Yields about 3 quarts.

fall

93

Butternut Squash Pie

Matthew Patterson, 4-H Club Member

1 1/2 cups of butternut squash
3/4 cup of sugar
1/2 teaspoon of salt
1 1/4 teaspoon of ground cinnamon
1/2 teaspoon of ginger
1/2 teaspoon of nutmeg
1/2 teaspoon of cloves
3 eggs, slightly beaten
1 1/4 cups of milk
1 6-ounce can of evaporated milk
plain pastry (recipe follows)

Peel, chunk and simmer the squash until tender.
Cool.

Combine the squash with the sugar, salt and spices.
Blend in the eggs, milk and evaporated milk and mix
well. Pour into a 10-inch pastry shell and bake at
400°F. for 50 minutes.

PLAIN PASTRY

This makes enough for a 10" double-crust pie:

2 cups of sifted flour
1 teaspoon of salt
2/3 cup of shortening
6 to 7 tablespoons of cold water

Mix the flour and salt. Cut in the shortening with a
pastry blender or blending fork til the pieces are the
size of small peas. Sprinkle water, a tablespoon at
a time, over the mixture, gently mixing with a fork.
Gather up the dough with your fingers, form into a
ball and divide in half. (You can wrap and refrigerate one half if you won't be using it)

Flatten the dough and roll out to a circle 1 inch larger than the pie pan you're using.

fall

94

Fresh Chopped Apple Cake

Jane Paulsen

1 cup of oil
2 cups of sugar
2 eggs
2 1/2 cups of flour
2 teaspoons of baking powder
1 teaspoon of soda
1/2 teaspoon of salt
1 teaspoon of vanilla
3 cups of chopped apples

Preheat your oven to 350°F.

Mix the oil and sugar together. Add the eggs and beat well. Sift the dry ingredients together and stir into the egg mixture. Add the vanilla and chopped apples.

Pour into a 9" x 13" greased cake pan and bake for 45 minutes. Serve warm with cream.

Easy Moist Apple Cake

Paul Vossen, Farm Advisor

2 cups of sugar
2 cups of flour
1 teaspoon of cinnamon
1/2 teaspoon of salt
1 teaspoon of baking soda
1/2 cup of butter, melted
1 teaspoon of vanilla
3 eggs
5 cups of chopped raw apples (peeled or unpeeled)
1 cup of raisins (optional)

Preheat the oven to 350°F. Mix the dry ingredients together thoroughly. Add the melted butter, vanilla, eggs, apples and raisins. Mix well.

Pour into a 9" x 16" greased cake pan and bake for 45 minutes (test for doneness with a toothpick - if inserted in the center it will come out clean if done).

Serves 10-12.

fall

Persimmon Pudding

Bruce Neidorf, Grower

1/4 cup of hulled raw sunflower seeds
1/4 cup of raw sesame seeds
5 or 6 soft ripe peeled Hachiya persimmons
2 peeled bananas
1 lime
1 lemon
1/2 pound of raisins
1/4 cup of shredded coconut (unless the
   granola has it already)
1 1/2 to 2 cups of granola-type cereal
1 pint of yogurt

(These amounts are approximate. I never measure anything when mixing up this pudding.)

Combine sunflower and sesame seeds and dry roast in a cast iron skillet on very low heat, stirring until well browned. Set aside to cool. In a large bowl, mash together the persimmons and bananas. Squeeze the lemon and lime and add the juice to the mashed fruit. Add raisins, coconut, granola, 1/2 of the yogurt and 3/4 of the roasted seeds. Mix well. Smooth the remainder of the yogurt over the top and

sprinkle with the remaining seeds. Cover and refrigerate overnight.

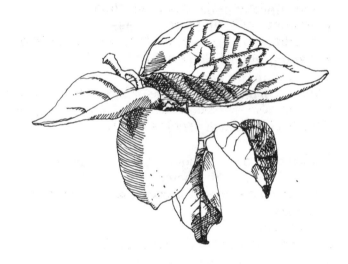

fall

96

Cheesecake with Kiwifruit

Helen Crowder, Grower

CRUMB CRUST:

1 cup of graham cracker crumbs
3 tablespoons of sugar
3 tablespoons butter or margarine, melted
1 tablespoon of lemon juice

Combine all ingredients well and press onto the bottom and sides of a buttered 9-inch spring-form pan. Bake at 350°F. for 10 minutes. Cool.

FILLING:

2 1/2 pounds cream cheese (at room temperature)
1 cup sugar
2 teaspoons grated lemon peel
1 teaspoon vanilla
3 tablespoons flour
5 eggs plus 2 egg yolks
1/4 cup light cream
3 kiwifruit

Preheat the oven to 475°F. Beat together the cream cheese, sugar, lemon peel and vanilla. Sprinkle the flour over the mixture and blend thoroughly. Add the eggs and yolks, one at a time, mixing well after each addition. Beat in the cream. Turn into the prepared crust and bake for 10 minutes. Reduce the heat to 250°F. and bake for 1 hour and 15 minutes. Remove from the oven and cool for 15 minutes. Spread with sour cream topping (recipe follows), return to the oven and bake at 475°F. for 5 additional minutes. Chill for several hours or overnight before serving. At serving time, peel and slice the three kiwifruit and arrange the slices on top.

SOUR CREAM TOPPING:

1 pint of sour cream
6 tablespoons of sugar
1 teaspoon of vanilla

Blend these well and pour over the baked cheesecake before re-baking and chilling.

fall

Persimmon Cup

Pat Summers

4 large Hachiya persimmons
3/4 cups of sugar
1 tablespoon of fresh lime juice
1 teaspoon of fresh lemon juice
2/3 cup of heavy cream, whipped
1 1/2 tablespoons of crystallized ginger,
   finely chopped

Peel, mash and push the pulp of the persimmons through a strainer. You'll need 2 cups (about 4 large, soft persimmons). Stir in the sugar, lime juice and lemon juice. Fold in the whipped cream, then taste. Adjust the sweetness to your own taste.

Spoon into individual serving dishes and top each serving with a sprinkling of ginger.

The two main types of persimmon you're likely to find are Hachiyas and Fuyus. Hachiyas are the pointy ones, which need to be nice and soft before trying to eat them, else you'll never get your mouth open again. Fuyus are more rounded, and can be eaten crisp.

fall

98

Prune Cake

Vivien Ecklund

1/2 cup of butter
1 cup of sugar
3 eggs, separated
1 cup of unsweetened stewed prunes, chopped finely
1 cup of prune juice
2 cups of cake flour
1/2 teaspoon of salt
1 teaspoon of nutmeg
1 teaspoon of cinnamon
1 teaspoon of ground cloves
1 teaspoon of baking powder
2 teaspoons of baking soda
1 tablespoon of water

Preheat your oven to 375° F.

Cream the butter and sugar together. Add the egg yolks, one at a time, beating well between each. Add the finely chopped prunes and juice and set aside. Beat the egg whites in a small bowl until soft peaks form. Sift the flour with the salt, spices and baking powder and set aside a teaspoonful of this mixture. Add the rest of it, a little at a time, to the prune mixture, mixing well after each addition. Dissolve the baking soda in the water and mix in the teaspoonful of flour. Add this to the prune mixture. Fold in the beaten egg whites and mix gently until just blended.

Pour into a sheet pan or 2 layer pans and bake for 40 minutes (for the sheet pan) or 30 minutes (for the 2 layer pans). Cool and cover with whipped cream, caramel icing, or seven-minute icing.

"Prunes are our regular friends."
— Paul Mancini

Pecan Pie

Art Davis, Grower

3 eggs, slightly beaten
1 cup of light or dark corn syrup
1 cup of sugar
2 tablespoons of butter or margarine,
   melted
1 teaspoon of vanilla
1 1/2 cups of pecans
1 unbaked 9" pastry shell

Preheat your oven to 350°F.

In a large bowl, stir together the first 5 ingredients until well blended. Stir in the pecans and pour into the pastry shell.

Bake for 50 to 55 minutes or until a knife inserted halfway between the center and edge comes out clean. Cool before serving.

Serves 8.

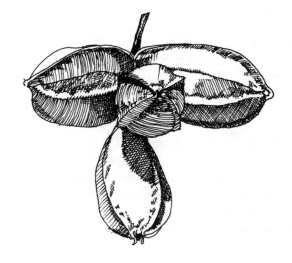

fall

Zwetschgendatschi

for Lee James from Elanore in West Germany

To save time in pitting the prunes for this recipe, you may want to cut them in halves and arrange then on the pastry in rows cut side down, next row pit side up. The pits can easily be removed after baking when still warm.

3 cups of flour
1 cup of sugar
3/4 cup of butter
salt to taste
1 egg
1-2 tablespoons of milk

3-4 cups of sliced fresh french prunes
1 teaspoon of cinnamon or to taste
1/2 cup of sugar or to taste

Preheat your oven to 350°F.

Process the flour, sugar, butter and salt with a food processor or blender or a fast fork until crumbly. Add the egg and enough milk to make a soft dough. Knead a bit and spread the dough onto a greased cookie sheet (10" x 14").

Pit and slice the prunes in halves or fourths. Arrange them on top of the dough in some appealing pattern. Sprinkle some cinnamon and sugar on top and bake for 20 minutes. The pastry should be soft -- don't overbake.

Although most people outside of California are only familiar with the dried version, fresh prunes (a form of plum) are becoming more well-known.

fall

WINTER

"Pruning, burning and general preparation for the new crops in the coming year -- this was, and is, the schedule for the traditional farmer in winter. The burning of brush left a strong scent of smoke in the chilly, frost-bitten morning air. Many orchards and gardens are asleep, patiently waiting to come alive once again in the spring."

- Dana McIntosh

Sorrel Soup

Rudy Marcus

1 bunch of Farmers Market sorrel
1/4 cup oil or butter for frying
1 quart of water
2 small red or 1 medium baking potato
4 chicken bouillon cubes

Wash the sorrel and chop the leaves coarsely.
Place in a pot or frying pan (enamelled or stainless)
with the oil or butter, heat and stir until just wilted; set
aside.

Cut the potatoes into small cubes without peeling
them. Add the potatoes and bouillon cubes to the
water and boil until the potatoes are tender. Drain
the potato cubes, reserving the broth.

Puree the potatoes in a blender or food processor,
mix with the reserved broth, and heat to the boiling
point. Add the warmed wilted sorrel; heat up to
serve, but do not boil.

winter

Mushroom, Leek and Eggplant Soup

Chef Kirby Tubb, Plaza Grill

2 ounces of butter or margarine
2 medium onions
4-6 garlic cloves
1 pound of mushrooms
1 bunch of leeks
1 medium eggplant
3 cups of chicken broth
2 cups of heavy cream, half & half or whole
   milk
1 cup of white wine
1/4 cup roux (2 tbls melted butter & 2 tbls
   flour, combined until smooth)
salt and pepper

Coarsely chop the onions; mince the garlic; wash and slice the mushrooms. Wash and trim the leeks, reserving the white part and part of the leaves. Dice the eggplant with the skin on.

Melt the butter in a large pot, add all vegetables and saute over medium heat until browned. Stir frequently while cooking to avoid scorching. Add enough water or chicken stock to cover the vegetables and simmer until tender (about one hour). Cool slightly, then puree in a blender.

Reheat the vegetable puree and add the cream, wine, and salt and pepper to taste. Bring it almost to a boil, then add the roux, stirring constantly until the soup has thickened slightly and the flour taste has disappeared. Adjust the seasonings to your own taste and serve.

winter

Potato-Leek Soup

Ursula Crane

3 cups of chicken broth, plus 2 cups water
2 leeks (using 3/4 of the stalk)
2 large red potatoes
4 tablespoons of parsley, chopped finely
4 cloves of garlic, pressed
3 tablespoons of safflower or olive oil
salt and pepper to taste
a splash of sherry
nutmeg to taste

Begin by starting to warm up the 5 cups of liquid in a soup kettle (just put it on low and let it get hot while you do the rest of the preparation).

Slice the leeks lengthwise into halves and wash them well with warm water. Chop them into 1/4-inch pieces. Scrub the potatoes with a brush (do not peel) and chop them into smaller-than-bite-sized pieces.

Using a cast iron skillet, heat the oil and add the leeks, potatoes, parsley and garlic. Saute for 4 to 5 minutes. Splash with sherry and add the spices to taste. Meanwhile back at the soup pot, the liquid should be hot, but not boiling. Add the potato/leek mixture and simmer for one hour.

The leek is the national emblem of Wales.

Winter

106

Kiwi and Spinach Salad

Beth Greenwald

3 cups of fresh spinach
2 cups of red-leaf lettuce
1 cup of arugula, dandelion or mustard
  greens
3 tablespoons of safflower oil
3 tablespoons of fresh lemon juice
2 tablespoons of honey
1 garlic clove, slivered
salt to taste
freshly ground white pepper
1 large kiwifruit, peeled & sliced
1 small red onion, sliced thin & separated
  into rings

Remove any thick stems from the spinach, lettuce and greens. Wash all and dry them in a salad spinner or pat them dry with paper towels. Tear the greens into bite-sized pieces and place them in a salad bowl; cover with a damp paper towel, plastic wrap and refrigerate.

In a small bowl, combine the oil, lemon juice, honey, garlic, salt and white pepper to taste; set this aside.

Just before serving, remove the garlic from the dressing. Toss the greens with the dressing, divide them among four individual bowls, and garnish them with the sliced kiwifruit and onion. I sometimes garnish with pieces of walnut also.

Serves 4.

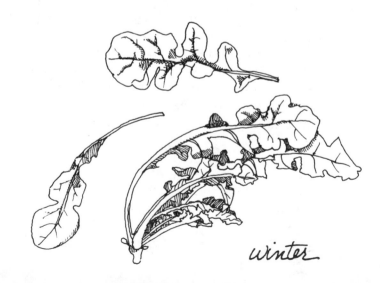

winter

107

Spinach Salad, California Style

Jack and Vanessa Henderson

3 quarts of fresh spinach, washed and torn
2 tablespoons of Romano or Parmesan
   cheese, grated
3 tablespoons of cooked crumbled bacon
1/4 cup of California sherry
1/3 cup of vegetable oil
3 tablespoons of chopped onions or
   shallots
1/4 teaspoon of seasoning salt
1/4 teaspoon of crumbled tarragon leaves
1/4 teaspoon of freshly ground black pepper

Dry the spinach and sprinkle with grated cheese
and crumbled bacon. Combine the remaining ingredients in a saucepan and bring to a boil. Pour over
the spinach, tossing well. Serve immediately.

Classic Vinaigrette Dressing

Mix together 1 part red wine vinegar and 3 parts olive, peanut or other vegetable oil. Add 1 tablespoon
of minced green onion, 1/4 teaspoon of crushed oregano and salt and pepper (freshly ground pepper if
possible) to taste. Sample for the proper balance of
vinegar and oil -- adjust to taste.

Season with other ingredients appropriate to the
salad, including Dijon mustard, crushed or minced
garlic, crushed tarragon or sweet basil (experiment!). Combine these with the oil and vinegar at
the last moment, to taste.

winter

Broccoli Salad

Georgia Peter, Grower

2 bunches of broccoli, cut up
2 cups of fresh mushrooms, sliced
4 eggs, hard-cooked and chopped
2 8-ounce cans of water chestnuts, sliced

DRESSING:

1/3 cup ketchup (try our recipe! page 147)
3/4 cup of sugar
1/4 cup of vinegar
2 tablespoons of Worcestershire sauce
1/2 teaspoon of salt
1 medium onion, quartered
1 cup of salad oil

Mix the dressing ingredients together in a blender.
Toss with the combined vegetables and serve cool.

Broccoli, like other members of the cabbage family, are thought to be useful in preventing certain kinds of cancer.

Broccoli and Cauliflower Salad Mix

Start to make this 3-4 hours before serving time.

2 bunches of broccoli flowerettes
1 head of cauliflower, cut up
4 greens onions, chopped, with tops
2 cups of cherry tomatoes (whole)

DRESSING:

1 cup of mayonnaise
1/2 cup of sour cream
1 tablespoon of vinegar
2 tablespoons of sugar
salt and pepper to taste

Mix the dressing ingredients well and pour over the combined vegetables. Marinate for 3-4 hours before serving.

winter

109

German Beef Rolls with Red Cabbage

Jurgen K.A. Wiese, California Master Chef

4 large slices (approximately 1/4" thick)
  beef top round
salt and pepper to taste
2 teaspoons of mustard
4 slices of lean bacon, cut in half
1 medium onion, sliced and sauteed
8 dill pickle chips
au jus, or water with beef seasoning
roux (see page 8)

1-1/2 pounds of red cabbage
1/4 cup of red wine vinegar
2 tablespoons of sugar
1 Gravenstein apple
salt and pepper to taste
1 bay leaf
a pinch of ground cloves
1 medium onion
butter or oil

Place the beef slices on a cutting board, season with salt, pepper and 1/2 teaspoon of mustard on each; place 1/2 a bacon strip, a few sauteed onions and 2 pickle chips in the center of each and roll up the slices. Secure them with a wooden toothpick. Brown the rolls in a casserole on all sides. Add au jus or water with beef seasoning and braise until the meat is tender. Remove the meat and reduce the stock over medium heat to the proper amount for 4 people; thicken with roux.

Quarter and remove the trunk from the cabbage; slice it very thin as for cole slaw. Mix the cabbage with salt, pepper, sugar, bay leaf, cloves and vinegar. Compress in a bowl and let marinate for 3-4 hours or even a day. Smother the sliced onion in butter; to it add the cabbage, thin slices of apple and a little liquid (stock or water). Cook in a saucepan until everything is tender, then check that the seasoning's to your taste. Serve with beef rolls, mashed potatoes or noodles.

Serves 4.

winter

Leeky Chicken

Rudy Marcus

2-1/2 pounds of Farmers Market leeks, of
medium diameter
4 boneless chicken breasts, skinned
1/4 cup of oil or butter for frying
salt and pepper

Wash the leeks well and cut them into four-inch
lengths.

Brown the chicken breasts over high heat in a skillet
(one or two minutes per side); salt and pepper them.
Add the leeks and cover tightly, lowering the heat
when steam is escaping the pan in a steady jet.
Braise for 10 minutes or until the leeks are tender.

Serve with pan juices, which will be slightly thickened naturally.

Serves 4.

At the turn of the century, it was estimated that nine-tenths of people living in or near Petaluma were raising poultry. The number of eggs being produced at that time is estimated to have been in the tens of millions of dozens.

Moo-Goo-Gay-Pan

Chef Steve Ly, Peking Gardens

12 ounces of chicken breast meat, in 3/8" x
   1" x 1" pieces
6 ounces of button mushrooms
1 tablespoon of oil
1 teaspoon of minced fresh garlic
3 ounces of onion, cut into 1" x 1" pieces
10 ounces of chicken broth
2 tablespoons of oyster sauce
2 tablespoons of cornstarch, mixed with 3
   ounces of chicken broth

Cook the chicken and mushrooms in boiling water
for one minute and remove. Set them aside.

Heat a tablespoon of oil in a wok or saucepan. Put
in the garlic and onion and stir-fry for 10 seconds,
then put in the chicken and mushrooms and stir-fry
for another 20 seconds. Finally, pour in the chicken
broth and oyster sauce. Add the cornstarch mixture
a little at a time, stirring, until the sauce thickens.

Serves 4-6.

winter

"If one more person asks me if my
onions are sweet I'm going to
scream! Of course they are; not
sweet like a candy bar but
sweet like an onion."
—Paula Mone

Johnson's Chicken with Orange

Johnson's Alexander Valley Wines

1 cup of orange marmalade
3/4 cup of Johnson's Pinot Noir
3/4 cup of water
1/2 cup of orange juice
1 8-oz can of apricots, drained & pureed
2 tablespoons of red currant jelly
2 tablespoons of brown sugar
2 tablespoons of cornstarch
1/4 cup of cold water

6 8-ounce chicken breast halves, skinned,
  boned and lightly floured
1/2 cup of flour
salt and pepper
oil

1/4 cup of sherry
1/4 cup of brandy
halved apricots and chopped fresh parsley

Combine the first 7 ingredients in a saucepan and simmer gently over low heat, stirring frequently until well blended. Slowly add the cornstarch, dissolved in the 1/4 cup of water, stirring constantly. Simmer the sauce until thickened, about 5 minutes.

Meanwhile, dredge the chicken breasts lightly in flour seasoned with salt and pepper. Heat some oil in large skillet, add the chicken and saute until golden brown on both sides; do not overcook. Drain on paper towels. Pour off the oil and wipe out the skillet.

Return the chicken to the pan, add the sherry and brandy and simmer 2 minutes. Stir in the apricot sauce, spooning it over the chicken to coat lightly. Transfer to a heated platter and garnish with apricot halves and chopped parsley. Serve with the remaining sauce.

Serves 6.

Plum Lemon Ginger Chicken Wings

Bill & Ellen Adamson, Happy Haven Ranch

3 pounds of chicken wings
2 tablespoons of soy sauce or tamari
1 jar of Happy Haven Plum Lemon Ginger
　Jam

Preheat your oven to 350°F.

Place the wings in a large oiled baking pan.
Sprinkle soy sauce or tamari over them. Bake them
for 30 minutes or until almost done. Spread jam
over wings, turning them to completely cover them.
Return them to the oven 'til the jam bubbles, 5 to 10
minutes.

Serves 6-8.

winter

114

Red Snapper Fillets with Greenhouse Greens

Jack and Vanessa Henderson, Growers

1 small head of bok choy (about 1 1/4 lb.)
12 mushrooms, cut in half
1 teaspoon of fresh thyme
1/4 cup of butter
1 cup of chicken or vegetable stock
1 1/2 pounds of red snapper fillets
2 teaspoons of cornstarch, mixed with
   1/2 cup of sour cream
1 tablespoon of fresh chopped dill
2 tablespoons of lemon juice

Separate the bok choy stalks, wash, slice the leaves off; cut the stalks crosswise into 1" pieces and the leaves into strips 1/4" wide. Saute the stalks, mushrooms and thyme in 2 T. butter for 5 minutes. Add half of the stock and cook uncovered until most of the liquid evaporates.

Divide the snapper into pieces and place skin side up in a buttered casserole. Bake at 400°F. until flesh is opaque and beginning to flake (20 minutes). Whilst the fish is baking, saute the bok choy leaves in the remaining butter until tender (1-2 minutes).

Do not brown them. Over low heat, stir the sour cream mixture into the cooked bok choy leaves, heat and thin with the remaining stock until it's a creamy sauce. Add the dill and keep it warm. When your fish is done, sprinkle a tablespoon of lemon juice over it and stir the other tablespoon into the stalk-and-mushroom mix. Surround the fish with the vegetables, pour the sauce over, and serve.

Serves 6.

winter

115

Curried Cauliflower and Spinach

Lotus Bakery

1 onion, chopped
3 tablespoons of oil and/or butter
1" of fresh ginger, grated, or 2 teaspoons
   powdered
1 1/2 teaspoons garlic, fresh or granulated
1 teaspoon of turmeric
2 teaspoons of cumin
1/3 teaspoon of cinnamon
2/3 teaspoon of cardamom
1 jalapeno chili, chopped
1 large head of cauliflower, cut up
1 1/2 cup of fresh tomatoes, chopped
1 large bunch of spinach, washed and
   tough stems removed
salt to taste

Saute the onion in the oil. Add the next seven ingredients and saute for several minutes more. Add the
cauliflower and the tomatoes and cook until soft.
Add the spinach and cook until it's soft. Salt to taste.

Serve with hot steamed rice and chutney.

winter

For a change of pace some time, look for the new purple variety of cauliflower.

Squash Patties

Bob and Jo Kearns, Growers

2 medium squash, grated
1 medium onion, grated
1 egg
1/2 cup of pancake mix, or so
salt and pepper to taste
1-2 tablespoons of oil

Mix together the squash, onion and egg and enough pancake mix to make a medium thick batter (about a half-cup). Add salt and pepper to taste. Pour pattie-sized amounts into a skillet and fry in oil until golden brown on both sides.

Makes 8 medium patties.

winter

Broccoli Pie

Rudy Marcus

Serve this as a main course for dinner, accompanied by garlic bread and a crisp green salad. It is also spectacular for brunch.

1 1/2 pounds of Farmers Market broccoli
1/4 cup of all-purpose flour
1/2 teaspoon of baking powder
1/2 teaspoon of dried, powdered oregano
1/4 teaspoon of salt
1 cup of sour cream
1 cup of cottage cheese
2 eggs
1/4 cup of butter or margarine, melted
1 large or 2 medium tomatoes, thinly sliced
1/4 cup of Parmesan or aged jack cheese,
   grated

Preheat the oven to 350°F.

Cut up the broccoli and steam it until crisp tender; arrange it on the bottom of a greased 9-inch pie plate. Combine the flour, baking powder, oregano, and salt in a mixing bowl; add the sour cream and

mix well. Add the cottage cheese, eggs, and melted butter; beat until nearly smooth and pour over the broccoli. Top with tomato slices and sprinkle grated cheese all over. Bake for an hour, or until a knife inserted near the center comes out clean.

Let it stand for 10 minutes before serving.

winter

118

Pasta a la Oje

Ray and JoAnne Fishman

This is great served hot or cold.

2 cups of tomatoes, diced in large pieces
2-3 cups of broccoli flowerettes (1" of stem
  is okay)
1 onion, finely diced
garlic (pressed) to taste
salt, pepper and oregano to taste
1 pound of spaghetti, cooked
1/2 to 1 cup of freshly grated Parmesan or
  Romano cheese
butter, at least 1 cube

Combine the tomatoes, broccoli, onion, garlic and
spices in a casserole dish or microwave bowl.
Steam until tender (with a little water) on the stove-
top or cook for 6 minutes in the microwave. Drain.

In a serving pot, layer the cooked spaghetti and vegetable mixture, putting a pat of butter between each
layer until you run out of both. Layer on the cheese
and reheat everything until it's all hot and bubbly.
Serve with fruit salad and garlic bread.

We loved this dish! Be careful
not to overcook the broccoli
(like we did). You want it to
be nice and green after
reheating.

winter

119

Soul Food Arabe

Rose Salem

In this dish, kale, mustard greens or collards may be substituted for chard. It is usually served accompanied by a cucumber and tomato salad.

2 large bunches of chard
1/2 cup of fine cracked bulgar wheat
1/4 cup of vegetable oil
1/2 of a medium onion, chopped
1 15-ounce can of "dry" blackeyed peas
    (no meat added)
salt and pepper

Wash, drain and chop the chard. Fill a 2-quart kettle about 1/3 full of water and bring it to a rolling boil. Add the chard, return to a boil, then lower the heat. Cook uncovered for about 5 minutes, stirring occasionally. Midway in this process, add the cracked wheat and stir to keep the kernels separated. Pour gently into a sieve or colander.

Using the same kettle, saute the onion in the oil for a few minutes. Add the chard mixture and the black eyed peas, season to taste with the salt and pepper and stir-fry over medium heat for five minutes.

Serves 4.

This is a traditional Syrian main dish.

winter

120

Spinach Timbales

Chef Josef Keller, La Province Restaurant

1 medium onion, chopped
2 ounces of butter
4 bunches of fresh spinach
Worcestershire, soy sauce, salt & pepper to
  taste
2 eggs
1/4 cup of cream
1 tablespoon of Parmesan cheese, grated
1 teaspoon of cornstarch

Preheat the oven to 350° F. Glaze the onions in the butter. Add the spinach, seasoning, and a small amount of water and blanch. Remove and chop it well.

Mix the eggs, cream, cheese and cornstarch with a whisk, then add the spinach and mix well. Fill buttered forms 3/4 full and bake in a water bath for 45 minutes.

Serves 6.

A timbale is sort of a cross between a custard and a souffle, baked in little individual molds (or as close as you can get, given your current kitchen inventory). To prevent burning, they're baked in a water bath -- place the filled forms in a shallow pan of hot water so that the water comes at least two-thirds of the way up their sides.

Winter

Baked Vegetable and Cream Cheese Casserole

Faye Zimmerman

"I've given a range of measurements for all ingredients because everything depends on the vegetables you use and your individual tastes. No other seasonings are necessary. This dish adds zest to any meal with poultry or meat or it can be served as a main vegetarian dish. Serve hot and enjoy!"

1 pound or more of mixed fresh vegetables*, chopped
8 ounces of chopped spinach (or half the amount of vegies)
1/4 - 1/3 cup of milk
2-4 tablespoons of butter or margarine
8 ounces of cream cheese
1/2+ pound of fresh mushrooms
1/2 - 1 package of dry onion soup mix
1/2 cup of Parmesan cheese, grated

*for a variety of colors and textures

Steam all of the vegetables to the first point of crunchiness and drain thoroughly. Meanwhile, heat/melt together the milk, butter, cream cheese, mushrooms and onion soup mix.

Preheat the oven to 325°F. Mix the thoroughly drained vegetables and heated cream cheese mixture; pour into a baking dish (whatever size you need!) with its sides and bottom greased. Sprinkle the top with grated parmesan or other tasty cheese. Cover and bake for 30 minutes or until it bubbles.

Serves 6-8.

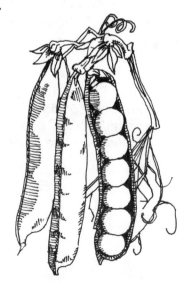

winter

122

Creamed Leeks

Bob Cannard, Grower

1 1/2 to 2 pounds of leeks
2 tablespoons of melted butter
2 tablespoons of flour
1 cup of milk
a pinch of nutmeg
a pinch of salt
a pinch of pepper
1/4 cup grated dry Monterey Jack cheese

Wash the leeks well and cut them into disks 1/4-inch thick. Put them into a skillet large enough so that they're not piled up too thickly. Cover them with a half-inch of water and simmer until they're barely tender. Don't boil them to mush!!

While the leeks are cooking, make a cream sauce by whisking together the melted butter, flour, milk and spices. Preheat the oven to 350° F.

Drain the leeks well in a colander. Put them into a buttered ovenproof baking dish, pour the cream sauce over and mix well. Sprinkle the cheese over the top and bake for 10 to 15 minutes.

Serves 6.

Leeks -- do they?

winter

Raspberry Hollandaise

Michele Jordan, Kozlowski Farms

This hollandaise sauce is made in a blender and produces excellent results:

3 egg yolks
2 tablespoons of Kozlowski Farms Black
   Raspberry Vinegar
1/2 teaspoon of fresh lemon juice
1/4 teaspoon of salt
pinch of sugar
1/2 cup of butter

Place the yolks, vinegar, lemon juice, salt and sugar in a blender. Heat the butter until bubbling. Cover the blender and turn on "high". Blend for 5 seconds, then remove the lid (with blender still blending) and pour the melted butter in a steady stream over the egg mixture. By the time all of the butter has been poured in, about 30 seconds, the sauce should be finished. To hold the sauce until serving time, immerse the blender container in warm water. Should the sauce become too cool, it can be warmed over a double boiler.

winter

Sauce for Sauteed Vegies

Paula Mune, Rocky Creek Gardens

Saute or steam fresh Farmers Market vegies as you normally would. When they're half-cooked, whisk together and add this sauce to them:

1/2 cup of soy sauce
1/2 cup (or less) of sugar
juice of 1/2 of a lemon
1-2 teaspoons of finely chopped ginger
   root
a handful of chopped green onions
as much garlic as you like, crushed

If you like, use chicken and vegies. Cook them separately, then combine them with the sauce.

Banana Nut Bread

Roancy Aubin, Sonoma Berry Patch

1/2 cup of oil
2/3 cup of brown sugar, packed
3 eggs
2 cups of mashed ripe bananas
1-3/4 cups of whole wheat flour
1/2 cup of oat bran
1 teaspoon of baking soda
1/2 teaspoon of salt
2/3 cup of milk plus 3 tablespoons of cold
   water
1 teaspoon of vanilla
1 cup of coarsely chopped nuts

Preheat the oven to 350°F.

Cream the sugar and oil; add the eggs and bananas. Sift the dry ingredients together and stir into the banana mixture, adding alternately with milk. Add the vanilla and nuts.

Pour into one large loaf pan or three small ones. Bake for 1 hour.

Makes one large loaf (9" x 5" pan) or three small loaves (3" x 7"). This bread freezes well.

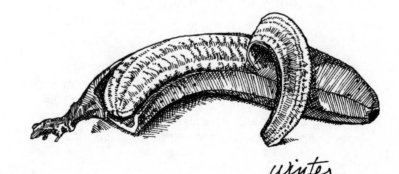

winter

Honey-Oatmeal Muffins with Orange Peel

Beth Greenwald

2/3 cup of milk
1/3 cup of vegetable oil
1 egg, beaten
1/4 cup of honey
1 1/2 cup of oats (quick or old-fashioned, uncooked)
1 teaspoon of cinnamon
1 cup of all-purpose flour
1/2 cup of raisins
1/2 cup of chopped nuts
1/3 cup of packed brown sugar
1 tablespoon of baking powder
3/4 teaspoon of salt
1 tablespoon of grated orange peel

Preheat your oven to 400°F.

Mix the milk, oil, beaten egg and honey together. Combine the remaining ingredients well in a mixing bowl and add the milk mixture to it, mixing until the dry ingredients are moistened. Fill 12 greased or paper-lined medium-sized muffin cups 2/3 full.

Bake for 15 to 18 minutes or until the muffins are golden brown.

Yields 1 dozen muffins.

Breads and cakes made with honey tend to stay moist longer than those made with only sugar as a sweetener. To measure honey easily, coat your measuring cup with salad oil -- the honey will slip right out.

winter

126

Key Lime Cake

Johnson's Alexander Valley Wines

1-1/3 cups of sugar
2 cups of all-purpose flour
2/3 teaspoon of salt
1 teaspoon of baking powder
1/2 teaspoon of baking soda
1 3-ounce package of lime-flavored gelatin
5 eggs
1-1/3 cups of cooking oil
3/4 cups of orange juice
1/2 teaspoon of vanilla
1 teaspoon of lemon extract

1/3 cup of Key lime juice (if unavailable,
   use regular limes)
1/3 cup of powdered sugar
whipped cream
lime slices

Preheat oven to 350°F.

Place the dry ingredients (including gelatin) into a mixing bowl. Add the eggs, oil, orange juice, vanilla and lemon extract. Beat until well blended. Pour the batter into a greased 9x13x2-inch pan; bake 25-30 minutes.

Remove the cake from the oven. Let it stand in the pan until almost cool, about 15 minutes. Prick the cake all over with a fork, then drizzle thoroughly with the lime juice mixed with the powdered sugar. Cover and refrigerate.

To serve, cut into squares, top with whipped cream and garnish with lime slices.

Makes 12-15 servings.

Key limes are small, round, thin-skinned limes that have their own distinct flavor.

winter

127

Friendship Cake

Joy Mathison, Grower

1 1/2 cups of STARTER (one cup of fruit
   juice plus 1/2 cup of brandy)
2 1/2 cups of sugar
1 quart of peaches, cut into cubes,
   including juice

Pour the above into a gallon jar. Put the lid on
loosely and stir daily for 10 days. DO NOT
REFRIGERATE. On the tenth day add:

1 1/2 cups of sugar and
1   3-ounce can of crushed pineapple

Stir daily for 10 days. On the twentieth day add:

1 1/2 cups of sugar and
2   9-ounce jars of maraschino cherries,
   drained and cut into quarters

Stir daily for 10 days. On the thirtieth day, bake 3
bundt cakes. For each cake you'll need the
following:

1 box of white or yellow cake mix
1 1/2 cups of the brandied fruit you've been
   making
2/3 cup oil
4 eggs
1 small package of vanilla instant pudding
1 cup of chopped nuts (optional)

Mix and pour into greased and floured pans. Bake
at 325°F. for 50 to 60 minutes. The leftover juice is
for 5 friends!!!

Winter

Lemon Mousse with Butter Pecan Crust

Kristin Brown, Kristin's Desserts

LEMON MOUSSE:

1 envelope of gelatin
1/4 cup of cold water
5 eggs, separated
3/4 cup of lemon juice
2 teaspoons of lemon zest

1 1/2 cups of sugar
1 cup of whipping
cream

Sprinkle the gelatin over the water and set it aside. Mix the egg yolks with the lemon juice, lemon zest and 3/4 cup of the sugar and place in a double boiler (make sure the water does not boil, or the eggs will curdle). Whisk the egg mixture constantly until it has a custard-like consistency (approx. 8 minutes). Remove from the heat, add the gelatin and mix well. Put in the freezer until it starts to set.

Whip the cream to soft peaks and set aside. Beat the egg whites gradually with the remaining 3/4 cup of sugar, just until the whites hold their shape. When the custard is ready, gently fold the egg whites and whipped cream into it. Pour this into the baked pastry (recipe below) and refrigerate for at least 6 hours before serving. Keep refrigerated.

PASTRY:

2 cups of flour
3/4 cup of sugar
1 ounce of pecans
1/2 cup plus 1 tablespoon of well-chilled
    unsalted butter

grated peel of 1 lime
1 egg

Combine 1 cup of flour with the sugar and pecans in a processor and mix to a fine powder. Transfer this to a large bowl and stir in the lime peel and remaining flour. Break the butter into small pieces and add it to the flour mixture; blend quickly with your fingertips until the mixture resembles coarse meal. Add the egg and continue mixing until the dough holds together. Don't overmix. Wrap it in plastic and refrigerate it for at least an hour.

Roll half of the dough on a lightly floured surface, then carefully press it into an 11-inch tart pan and prick the bottom with a fork. Chill for 30 minutes. Preheat the oven to 400 F. and bake the pastry shell until it's golden brown (10-12 minutes). Let it cool. Add the Lemon Mousse. Refrigerate.

Winter

Oatmeal Jam Squares

Carmen Kozlowski, Kozlowski Farms

2 cups of oatmeal
1 cup of flour
1/2 teaspoon of salt
1/2 teaspoon of baking soda
1/2 cup of chopped walnuts
1/2 cup of brown sugar
3/4 cup of melted butter
a 10 ounce jar of your favorite Kozlowski
  Farms Jam

Preheat your oven to 350°F.

Combine all ingredients except the jam and mix well. Set aside one cup of this mixture and spread the rest in the bottom of a greased 9" square pan. Bake for 10 minutes.

Spread the jam on top of the baked crust, up to the sides of the pan. Sprinkle the remaining crust mixture on top, then bake 20 minutes more or until the top is golden brown.

Cool in the pan and then cut into bars.

winter

Kozlowski Farms is a Sonoma County treasure. They produce a wide range of jams, jellies, vinegars, mustards, syrups and sauces ... every one a gem.

Buttermilk Coffee Cake

Supervisor Helen Rudee's Favorite Recipe

2-1/4 cups of sifted flour
1/2 teaspoon each of salt and cinnamon
1/2 cup of brown sugar, firmly packed
1/2 cup of granulated sugar
3/4 cup of salad oil
1 cup of walnuts, coarsely chopped
1 teaspoon of cinnamon
1 teaspoon of baking soda
1 teaspoon of baking powder
1 egg, slightly beaten
1 cup of buttermilk

Preheat the oven to 350°F. Sift the flour with the salt and 1/2 teaspoon of cinnamon into a large bowl. Add the brown sugar, granulated sugar and salad oil, and mix on medium speed until well-blended and feathery. Remove 3/4 cup of this mixture, add the nuts and the 1 teaspoon of cinnamon to it and mix; set aside for the topping.

To the remaining flour mixture, add the baking soda, baking powder, egg and buttermilk. Mix until smooth. Spoon the mixture into a buttered pan (9" x 13" x 2") and level off the top. Sprinkle the reserved topping evenly over the top and lightly press it in with the back of a spoon. Bake in a moderate oven (350 F., or 325°F. for a glass pan) for 25 to 30 minutes or until it tests done. Cut into squares; serve warm.

Makes 12 servings.

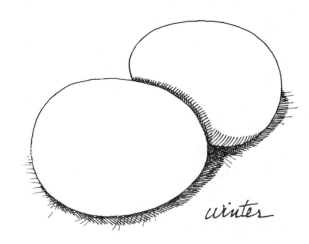

winter

131

Vanilla Pistachio Cake

Vahid Arjmand's Grandmother's Recipe

1 cup of butter
1 cup of sugar
4 eggs
1 cup of milk
2 teaspoons of vanilla
2 cups of flour
1 teaspoon of baking soda
1 cup of raw pistachios, chopped

Preheat the oven to 400° F.

Cream the butter with the sugar. Add the eggs, milk
and vanilla and blend well. Measure out the dry ingredients and add them to the wet ingredients.
Pour the batter into an oiled 9" x 9" pan, reduce the
oven heat to 350° F. and bake for 45 minutes.

Seal nuts in plastic bags and
store them in the freezer. They'll
stay fresh _much_ longer.

winter

Golden Cottage Pudding

Clarian Standing (Hilda's Mom)

1/2 cup of shortening
1-1/4 cups of sugar
2 eggs, separated
1-1/2 cups of grated carrot
3 teaspoons of baking powder
1/2 teaspoon of salt
1-1/2 cups of flour
1/4 cup of milk
1 teaspoon of lemon extract
Hot Pudding Sauce (recipe follows)

Preheat your oven to 350°F. Beat the egg whites to stiff peaks. Cream the shortening and sugar together. Add the egg yolks, one at a time, beating well after each. Add the grated carrots. Sift the flour, baking powder, and salt together and add alternately with the milk to the batter. Add the lemon flavoring and fold in the stiffly beaten egg whites. Pour into a greased 8" square pan and bake for 55-60 minutes. Serve with Hot Pudding Sauce.

Serves 8.

HOT PUDDING SAUCE:

1 cup of sugar
4 tablespoons of flour
1/4 teaspoon of salt
1-1/2 cups of boiling water
4 tablespoons of lemon juice
4 tablespoons of butter

Mix all of the ingredients well and heat in a double boiler. Serve over warm Golden Cottage Pudding.

winter

Nut and Graham Cracker Goodies

Joy Mathison, Grower

Graham crackers (1/4 to 1/2 a box)
2 cubes (8 ounces) of butter or margarine
2/3 cup of sugar, white or brown
1 cup of chopped nuts (your choice)

Preheat your oven to 350°F.

Lay as many graham crackers as will fit in the bottom of a cookie sheet. In a small saucepan, melt the butter and mix in the sugar. Pour over the graham crackers. Sprinkle with the nuts and bake for 7 minutes. Cool, then break up into bite sized pieces.

Terrific!

Hot Mulled Wine

Judy Collins, Grower

1/2 gallon of cranberry juice
1/2 gallon of fresh apple juice
1/2 gallon of Vin Rose Wine

1 cup of brown sugar
1 rounded tablespoon of whole cloves
8 sticks of cinnamon, broken up

Pour the juices and wine into a large automatic coffee percolator. Place the sugar, cloves and cinnamon in the basket and plug it in. (OR you can tie the spices in a cheesecloth bag and simmer them with the juices and wine in a large kettle) Let it all perk through a regular cycle --- and lo and behold, you have a yummy hot drink for the holidays! (And your house smells wonderful...the neighbors will be making excuses to come over to visit).

winter

CANNING, PRESERVING AND FREEZING

"Hot kitchens, hot pots, hot jars, fresh fruits and vegetables....tantalizing smells travelling from Mom's
kitchen. My fondest memory is of the hustle-bustle
of canning time. This was a family activity with every
family member participating. Canning provided a
means to enjoy the fresh fruits and vegetables of
every season on any day of the year."

- Dana McIntosh

Herb Vinegar Recipes

Ellyn Pelikan, Pelikan Spring Farm

Whaddya do with herbal vinegars anyway? You use them in some of the following: Stews, soups, mayonnaises, salad dressings, basting meats, fruit salads, vegetable dips, raw oyster and clam dips, added to club soda for a refreshing summer drink, cold pasta salads, cold cooked vegetables, facial washes and marinades. Recipes to savor:

- Mix cold pasta with chopped tomatoes, chopped olives, chopped green peppers and slivered leeks. Mix **basil vinegar**, oil, and crushed pepper to taste. Splash on the salad.

- Slice 1/4 cup of tomatoes, 1/4 cup of mozzarella cheese, olives and sweet red onions. Arrange this on a nice plate. Sprinkle with chopped basil. Splash on **basil** or **rosemary vinegar** and drizzle olive oil over all. Season to taste.

- 1 cup **each** of sliced: strawberries, cherries, and oranges; 1/2 cup of slivered almonds. Arrange the fruit on a plate. Scatter with almonds. Make a dressing of 3 teaspoons of **mint vinegar** and 1 table-spoon of sugar. Drizzle over the salad. Garnish with pansy petals.

- Mix 1/4 cup of **thyme** or **mixed herb vinegar**, 1 teaspoon **each** of minced ginger and garlic, and 1/2 teaspoon of cracked black pepper. Arrange some nice fish or chicken in a greased baking dish. Pour the herb mixture over all. Lay sprigs of rosemary or lemon thyme over the fish or chicken and bake at 350 until fork-tender.

- For a facial wash - dilute 2 tablespoons of **mint vinegar** with 1/2 cup of water. Splash on your clean face to preserve the acid mantle on your skin (that's a good thing!). Mix a fresh batch daily.

- A hair rinse of 3 tablespoons of **rosemary vinegar** and 2 cups of water is said to make a brunettes hair very shiny!

Have fun with these recipes! Experiment on your own. Savor and enjoy.

canning

138

Freezing Parsley and Bell Peppers

Marie Schutz

I pick parsley, wash it well and remove the tough stems, then drain it and squeeze to get as much water out as possible. Bag it in small ziploc bags which are compressed to form the parsley into cylinders about 4 inches long by 1 1/2 inches, then quick-freeze. When you want chopped parsley, take out a roll (do not thaw) and shave as much as is needed from the end of the roll. Return the package to the freezer at once, before it has a chance to thaw. This saves chopping, and keeps its flavor for many months.

I do the same with bell peppers. Cut them in strips after removing the seeds, bundle (red, green and yellow together sometimes) and freeze in small zip - loc bags. When you need to add peppers to casseroles (not to salads - the texture is changed by freezing) cut pieces off one end of the bundle, always remembering to return the big piece to the freezer before it has a chance to thaw.

Frozen Melon-Orange

Marie Schutz

When the cantaloupes finally begin to ripen, they often come on faster than they can be used. I save some as Frozen Melon-Orange:

Fresh cantaloupes
Frozen orange juice concentrate - almost thawed

Peel the cantaloupe and cut it into bite-sized pieces (use a melon baller, or cut it into cubes). Pack it into pint-size freezer containers. Pour over some frozen orange juice in its concentrated form. Fill container almost full, then place a piece of crumpled plastic wrap on top of the juice, to help keep the melon pieces submerged in the juice (if you try this once you'll get it). Cap the containers and mark the date, freeze them and use them within 4 months.

This makes a tasty dessert by itself (thawed, but with a little ice-crystal still present), and is also a wonderful base for a fruit compote for the holidays. Just add other fruits, berries, coconut or nuts for additional textures and colors.

canning

Dill Pickles

Helen Crowder, Grower

3 - 4 quart jars of cucumbers*
1 teaspoon of dill seed
2 to 4 cloves of garlic
2 to 4 red peppers (hot or sweet)
1 pint of vinegar
1/2 cup of salt
2 quarts of water
alum

Wash the cucumbers and let them stand overnight in cold water. Divide up and place the dill, garlic, and peppers into the jars and add the cukes. Boil together the vinegar, salt and water. Pour this over the cukes to cover them and then add 1/4 teaspoon of alum per jar. Put on the lids, and boil in a hot water bath for 5 minutes to seal.

Yields 3 to 4 quarts.

Always follow the lid manufacturers instructions when canning! No short-cuts! Botulism is no fun at all. canning

More Dill Pickles

Clarian Standing (Hilda's Mom)

a bunch of cucumbers (enough for 8 qts.) *
3 quarts of water
1 quart of 5 1/2% vinegar
1 cup of coarse salt (uniodized)
8 cloves of garlic
8 hot peppers
alum
16 heads of fresh dill
8 grape leaves

Chill the cucumbers. Distribute them amongst 8 quart jars (make sure you have new lids!). Bring to a boil the water, vinegar and coarse salt. While this is heating, put into each jar with the cukes: 1 clove of garlic, 1 hot pepper, a pinch of alum, and 2 heads of fresh dill. Press down and fill each jar to 1/2 inch from the top with the hot liquid. Place a grape leaf on top of each.

Put the lids on the jars and place them in a boiling water bath for 20 minutes. Be sure to cover the jars with water.

Jennifer's Pickled Jerusalem Artichokes

Jane Paulsen

You may also find jerusalem artichokes under the name of sunchokes. They're gnarly little brown roots that have a unique flavor all their own.

2 pounds of jerusalem artichokes
green peppers
onions
several dry red chili peppers
lemons
quart jars
1 quart of cider vinegar
1 tablespoon of dry mustard
1 tablespoon of powdered turmeric
1 tablespoon of mustard seed
1/2 tablespoon of celery seed
1 1/2 cup of white sugar
1/2 cup of brown sugar

Scrub, scrape and peel the artichokes and cut them into pieces. Mix up a supersaturated solution of salt and water (adding and mixing salt into a quart or two of warm water until added salt ceases to dissolve); put the artichokes into this solution and leave them there for 24 hours, then drain them and rinse well (they'll be soft).

Mix together the vinegar, spices and sugars and boil them for 20 minutes. In the meantime, into each bottling jar put:

> a slice of green pepper
> a slice of onion
> 1 dry red chili pepper
> a slice of lemon
> a bunch of artichokes to fill

When your vinegar mixture is ready, pour it over the chokes and seal the jars according to the lid manufacturers instructions.

canning

Bread and Butter Pickles

Bob and Jo Kearns, Growers

25-30 medium sized lemon cucumbers
8 large white onions
2 large sweet peppers
1/2 cup of salt
5 cups of cider vinegar
5 cups of sugar
2 tablespoons of mustard seed
1 teaspoon of turmeric
1/2 teaspoon of cloves

Wash the cucumbers and slice them as thin as possible. Chop the onions and peppers, and combine them with the cucumbers and salt. Let this stand for 3 hours. Drain.

Combine the vinegar, sugar, and spices in a large pan and bring to a boil. Add the drained cucumber mix and heat thoroughly but DO NOT BOIL. Pack while hot into sterilized jars and seal according to manufacturers instructions.

Makes about 8 pints.

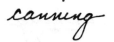
canning

Green Relish

Jessie Osborne Farlow

25 large cucumbers
6 green peppers
2 red peppers
8 onions
1 large bunch of celery

1 1/2 cups of water
2 handfuls of salt

Grind all of the vegetables together and add the water and salt. Let stand for 24 hours. Drain dry.

Make a syrup of:

2 ounces of mustard seed (2 2/3 tablespoons
1 1/2 ounces celery seed (2 tablespoons)
1 tablespoon of turmeric
2 quarts of vinegar
8 cups of white sugar

Bring the syrup to boil with the vegetable mix and add green food coloring if desired. Pour into pint jars and seal at once as directed by your lid manufacturer. Do not let cook -- just bring all to a boil.

canning

Zucchini Relish

Rose Arfsten

10 cups of zucchini, peeled, seeded and
  grated
4 cups of grated onions
5 tablespoons of salt
5 cups of sugar
2 cups of vinegar plus 1/4 cup of vinegar
1/4 teaspoon of pepper
1 tablespoon of turmeric
1 tablespoon of prepared mustard
2 teaspoons of celery salt
2 tablespoons of cornstarch

Mix together the vegetables and salt. Cover with water and let stand overnight. Drain, wash and drain again, and put them into a large pot.

Mix the sugar and 2 cups of vinegar. Make a paste of the 1/4 cup of vinegar, pepper, turmeric, mustard, celery salt, and cornstarch. Add this to the vinegar and sugar mixture, mix well and pour over the vegetables. Cook everything slowly for an hour.

Pour into hot jars and seal as directed by your lid manufacturer.

Makes about 7 pints.

canning

144

Yellow Crookneck Squash Relish

Jackie Robins, Grower

"This is really a great recipe to use up your abundant yellow crookneck squash. It looks very pretty in the jars and serves well as a condiment for your holiday meals. It's flavor is similar to bread and butter pickles."

5 **pounds of yellow crookneck squash (not peeled)**
6 **medium onions (chopped or ground)**
1/3 **cup of salt**
1 **sweet red pepper (chopped or ground)**
1 **green pepper (chopped or ground)**
1 **small hot pepper (optional)**
3 1/2 **cups of vinegar**
1 **tablespoon of cornstarch**
1 **tablespoon of turmeric**
1 **tablespoon of nutmeg**
1 **tablespoon of dry mustard**
2 **tablespoons of celery seed**

Chop or grind the squash. Cover with water, then drain in a colander (should measure 10 cups). Mix the squash and onion, add the salt, and let stand overnight.

Rinse in cold water and drain. Combine all remaining ingredients with the squash and onions in a large pot. Heat to boiling, then reduce the heat and simmer for 30 minutes. Pack in clean scalded jars and process in a boiling water bath for 10 minutes.

Yields 5 pints.

canning

Auntie Ann's Ketchup

Ditty Cannard, Grower

16 pounds of tomatoes
3 peeled onions

2 tablespoons salt
1/3 cup sugar
2 teaspoons celery salt
2 teaspoons dry mustard
1 teaspoon paprika

1 tablespoon whole allspice
1 tablespoon whole cloves
1 broken stick of cinnamon
2 cups cider vinegar

Chop the tomatoes and onions and put them in a kettle. Cook slowly until soft, then put it through a food mill and measure -- it should be about 4 quarts. Add the next 5 ingredients to the puree. Put the allspice, cloves and cinnamon in a little muslin bag (or in a tea holder) and add the bag at the same time as the other spices. Bring all to a boil and cook rapidly for 1 hour. Discard the spice bag. Add the 2 cups of vinegar and cook until thick. It will thicken

more when it cools. Seal in hot sterilized jars. It's best when aged for 2 to 3 months before using.

To cut the salty taste, add two chopped stalks of celery to the onions and tomatoes before cooking. For more of a steak sauce, use half red tomatoes and half green and leave the spice bag in until it's time to put the ketchup into jars.

Yields 6 to 8 pints.

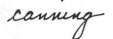

canning

146

Tomato Sauce

Betty Dericco

8 quarts of very ripe tomatoes, rinsed
1/4 cup of minced garlic
1/2 cup of lightly packed fresh oregano
  leaves
1/2 cup of chopped lightly packed fresh basil
3 tablespoons of wine vinegar
2 teaspoons of pepper
1 to 2 tablespoons of sugar
1 to 2 tablespoons of salt

Trim any spoilage from the tomatoes. Chop them coarse or fine (to your taste) and place them with their juice in a large pan (10-12 quarts). Add the garlic, oregano, basil, vinegar, pepper and 1 table-spoon each of sugar and salt, and bring to a boil over high heat. Reduce the heat to medium and boil gently, uncovered, stirring occasionally, until the mixture is reduced to 5 quarts (1-1/2 to 2 hours).

Scoop 3 to 4 cups of the mixture at a time into a food processor or blender and process until all is pureed. Return the tomato sauce to the pan and continue to cook uncovered over medium heat. Boil gently, stir-ring frequently, until the sauce is reduced to 4 quarts (30 to 40 minutes more). Add additional sugar and salt to taste if desired.

To Can: Ladle the boiling sauce into hot sterilized canning jars, leaving 1/4 inch headspace for pints and 1/2 inch headspace for quarts. Wipe the rim, put the scalded lids in place, and screw on the rings tightly. Set the jars on a rack in a deep kettle and add boiling water to cover. Bring the water to a sim-mer; simmer pints for 15 minutes, quarts for 20 min-utes. Lift the jars from the water and let cool.

Yields 4 quarts.

canning

Grandmother's Rose Sauce

Dana McIntosh

For this recipe, buy fresh cranberries the previous season and freeze them, because they are unavailable during apple season. This is a Harvest Fair ribbon-winner, and it looks absolutely beautiful in the jars.

25 apples
4 cups of brown sugar (or less if your apples are sweet)
1/2 of a fresh lemon
1 tablespoon of cinnamon
1 teaspoon of nutmeg
1 cup of frozen cranberries
2-3 cups of water

Wash, core and chop the apples (don't peel). Place them in a large sauce pan with the brown sugar, the juice of the 1/2 lemon, cinnamon, nutmeg and enough water to create a moist texture. Cook the ingredients until boiling. Mash the apple with a potato masher, then add the frozen cranberries. Reduce the heat, then continue to simmer for about 15 minutes.

Pour into sterilized quart jars and seal, then process in a hot water bath for a minimum of 20 minutes.

Yields 6 quarts.

Note: Remember to sample the fruit and add or delete spices to your own taste. The cranberries in this recipe give a rich warm rose color to the finished jars.

canning

148

Fuyu Persimmon Chutney

Chef John Ash, John Ash & Co.

"I look forward to late summer each year for the local Fuyu persimmons. Unlike their regular counterparts, Fuyus can be eaten fresh without pucker madness!"

2 firm Fuyu persimmons (5 ounces each)
2 tablespoons of minced red onion
2 teaspoons of olive oil
1 tablespoon of currants or golden raisins
1 tablespoon of dry sherry
1/2 teaspoon of chopped chives
1/2 teaspoon of rice wine vinegar

Dice the unpeeled Fuyus. Saute the onion in olive oil until it's soft but not brown, then remove from the heat to cool.

Gently heat the raisins and sherry together, then take them off the heat and allow the raisins to absorb the sherry.

Combine all cooled ingredients and refrigerate until serving time.

Apricot Sundaes

Sue Wood

2 cups of chopped fresh apricots
2 cups of sugar
1 tablespoon pure vanilla
2 ounces (1/4 cup) of bourbon (don't use brandy)

Mix the apricots and the sugar together well in a saucepan. Bring them to a boil and boil until they're soft -- about 5 or 10 minutes -- stirring frequently to prevent sticking. Remove the pan from the heat, add the vanilla and bourbon and mix well. Pour into sterilized jars or into plastic bags and freeze.

Serve by spooning about a tablespoon, still frozen, over your favorite vanilla or french vanilla (mmmmm) ice cream.

Apricots were first planted in California in the missions in the 1700s.

canning

Sweet Pepper Jam Appetizer

Jill Brown

Don't be put off by the name -- this creation is rather sweet and tangy, not hot at all. I make this at the end of summer when peppers are inexpensive. I like to make a batch of red and one of green. It's a great appetizer for the holidays!

4-1/2 pounds of sweet bell peppers (red is best but green is also good)
1 tablespoon of salt
2 cups of tarragon vinegar
3 cups of sugar

Remove the seeds from the peppers and grind them up (in a food processor if possible). Sprinkle them with the salt, mix and let stand for 2 hours. Drain.

Add the vinegar and sugar. Cook the mixture on high heat until it comes to a boil, then simmer uncovered for 3 1/2 to 4 1/2 hours, stirring occasionally, until it's the consistency of jam. Serve over cream cheese with crackers.

Yields 4 to 5 cups.

canning

Spicy Pepper Jam

Lee James, Tierra Vegetables

2 pounds of sweet peppers
1 pound of Jalapeno peppers
1 tablespoon of salt
3 3/4 cups of sugar
2 1/2 cups of white vinegar

Seed and remove the membranes from peppers using rubber gloves. Chop them finely, in a food processor if possible. Add the salt and cover with cold water. Let stand for one hour, drain and rinse.

Add the sugar and vinegar to the pepper mixture and boil gently until thick (about an hour, stirring occasionally).

Yields 6 to 8 pints.

Kiwi-Pineapple Jam

Helen Crowder, Grower

2 1/2 cups of chopped kiwifruit
2 cups of unsweetened crushed pineapple
1 tablespoon of lemon juice
1 box of pectin
2 1/2 cups of sugar
5 drops of green food coloring

Mix the kiwifruit, pineapple, lemon juice and pectin in a large saucepan and stir well. Bring to a boil and boil for 1 minute. Add the sugar all at once and bring the mixture to a full boil, one that cannot be stirred down, for 1 full minute, stirring constantly to prevent scorching. Add the food coloring last, stir and remove from heat. Skim and pour immediately into hot sterilized jars if desired.

Yields 4 to 5 half-pint jars.

Peach-Orange Preserves

Sandra Britt

12 large peaches, peeled
1 navel orange with skin
7-8 cups of sugar
1 pouch of Certo or other pectin

Peel and grind up the peaches and the orange (skin and all). Measure by the cupful into a large heavy dutch oven (not aluminum) -- it should be 7 to 8 cups. Measure an equal amount of sugar into the pot. Bring to a boil, stirring frequently to prevent scorching. When it boils, add one pouch of Certo and let it boil for 5 minutes, stirring frequently.

Pour into hot sterilized jars and seal. I decorate the jars and give some as gifts.

Yields 8 half-pint jars.

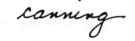
canning

Plums for A.J.

Dana McIntosh

The plums for this recipe may be pitted before canning, if desired. This was a ribbon-winner at the Harvest Fair.

9 cups of whole Satsume plums
French Cognac
Medium Syrup, boiled (1 cup of sugar and
**   2 cups of water, boiled)**

Wash the fruit, discarding damaged or overripe pieces. Divide the plums among hot pint canning jars, packing them full. Pour in 3/4 cup of French Cognac (more if desired). Fill the rest of each jar with the syrup, leaving 1/2" airspace. Remove bubbles, adding more syrup if necessary.

Seal the jars according to the lid manufacturers directions and process for 20 minutes in a boiling water bath. Cool, label and store in a cool location.

Yields 6 pints.

"Memories, memories! A charming Italian gentleman giving me a bag of Satsume plums - what could be more appropriate from an Italian, especially in matters of the heart? I took the plums, sweetened, spiced and canned them, and returned the gift to him. And guess what? He returned the jars!"

— Dana McIntosh

canning

Cherries Cointreau

Dana McIntosh

Another Harvest Fair ribbon winner:

4 pounds of dark sweet cherries (about 9 cups)
Cointreau liqueur
Medium Syrup, boiled (2 cups of water + 1 cup of sugar)

Stem, rinse and pit the cherries. Pack them into pint canning jars and add 3/4 cup of Cointreau. Add Medium Syrup to each jar until 1/2 " from the rim. Remove the bubbles. Seal the jars per the lid manufacturer's instructions and process for 20 minutes in a boiling water bath.

Cool, label and store in a cold place. Spoon them over vanilla ice cream, or eat them plain (plain??) as a dessert.

Yields 6 pints.

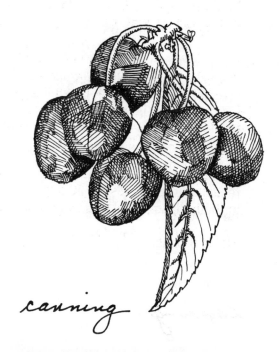

canning

Preserved Lemons

Chef John Ash, John Ash & Co.

6 ripe lemons, scrubbed (Eureka or Meyer
   preferred)
1 tablespoon of sugar
1/2 cup of sea salt
2/3 cup of lemon juice
1 1/2 cups of olive oil

Cut the lemons into 6 or 8 wedges each and toss
with the salt and sugar. Place them in a 1-quart
glass or plastic jar with a lid and pour the lemon
juice over. Close tightly and let it sit at room temperature for a week, shaking the jar every day to mix the
salt, sugar and lemons.

At the end of the week pour olive oil over and it can
be stored indefinitely refrigerated.

These don't really need to be refrigerated if you use
them regularly and up within a month or so. I use
them slivered in salad dressings (especially good
with extra virgin olive oil) and in fresh "chutneys" to
garnish grilled meats and fishes. One of my favorites is to use equal parts of slivered roasted red pepper, slivered preserved lemon and pitted/slivered
Kalamata olives all mixed with just a few drops of olive oil to top grilled chicken (local chicken of
course!).

canning

Christmas Grapes

Pat Summers

Prepare this in late September or early October for Christmas gifts.

Seedless grapes, red or green
Granulated sugar
Brandy

Remove the seedless grapes from their stems. Prick around the grapes, about 5 or 6 times each, with a thin bamboo skewer.

Fill a quart jar with grapes. Pour in granulated sugar, shaking it down, until the sugar comes halfway up the fruit. Then fill the jar with brandy, covering the grapes. Place the lid on the jar.

Mark the jar "To be opened" and a date about 3 months from the date packed.

canning

155

Apple Butter

Flora Early, Grower

12 pounds of apples
2 cups of water
3 cups of sugar
1 cup of cider vinegar
2 tablespoons of cinnamon

Peel and dice the apples (or better yet, invite a few friends over and peel and dice the apples together!). Cook the diced apples in the water until soft. Rub the soft apples through a food mill or sieve. Add the sugar, vinegar and cinnamon and mix well. Cook the apple butter over a low heat on top of the stove, stirring constantly, or in a roasting pan in a 375° F. oven, stirring every 15 minutes. Use a wooden spoon. With either method, cook and stir until the apple butter is as thick as you like it to be. Pour into sterilized jars and seal.

Nectarine Butter

Pat Summers

1/4 pound of sweet butter, softened
1-2 tablespoons of honey
a squeeze of lemon
nutmeg
2 small nectarines*

*You could also use peeled peaches or fresh strawberries

Beat the butter with the honey until smooth. Then beat in the squeeze of lemon and a few grains of nutmeg. Cut the fruit into pieces and, while beating, add 1 piece at a time. When all of the fruit has been incorporated (it won't be smooth), mound in a bowl, cover and chill. Serve with hot breads or on pancakes.

canning

INDEX

Appetizers
  Mustard Tart, 26
  Plum Lemon Ginger Chicken Wings, 114
  Sweet Pepper Jam Appetizer, 150
Apples
  Apple Bread, 91
  Apple Butter, 156
  Cabbage-Apple Slaw, 74
  Chicken Sebastopol, 78
  Easy Moist Apple Cake, 95
  Fresh Chopped Apple Cake, 95
  Grandmother's Rose Sauce, 148
  Lapin Gravenstein, 45
Apricots
  Apricot Sundaes, 149
  Sour Apricot & Raspberry Buckle, 67
  Sunshine Bars, 30
Artichokes, Jerusalem, 141
Asparagus
  Asparagus Beef w/ Oyster Sauce, 13
Avocado
  Avocado Chiffon Mousse, 32
Bananas
  Banana Nut Bread, 125
Beans
  Beans for Autumn, 82

Fava Bean Soup, 9
  Meatless Chili, 82
  Red Bean and Kale Soup, 9
Beef
  Asparagus Beef w/ Oyster Sauce, 13
  German Beef Rolls w/ Red Cabbage, 110
Berries. See individual berries
Beverages
  Hot Mulled Wine, 135
Bok Choy, 115
Breads
  Apple Bread, 91
  Banana Nut Bread, 125
  Honey-Oatmeal Muffins with Orange Peel, 126
  Oatmeal Raisin Bread, 27
  Pumpkin Bread, 91
  Raspberry Bread, 60
  Scones, 92
  Zucchini Bread, 61
Broccoli
  Broccoli & Cauliflower Salad Mix, 109
  Broccoli Pie, 118
  Broccoli Salad, 109
  Pasta a la Oje, 119
Cabbage

Cabbage Borsht, 70
  Cabbage-Apple Slaw, 74
  German Beef Rolls w/ Red Cabbage, 110
  Noodles and Cabbage, 21
  Stuffed Cabbage Rolls, 81
  Sweet and Sour Cabbage, 86
Cakes
  Buttermilk Coffee Cake, 131
  Carrot Cake, 33
  Cheesecake with Kiwifruit, 97
  Easy Moist Apple Cake, 95
  Fresh Chopped Apple Cake, 95
  Friendship Cake, 128
  Key Lime Cake, 127
  Lemon Chiffon Cake, 31
  Prune Cake, 99
  Vanilla Pistachio Cake, 132
Canning method, 147
Carrots
  Carrot Cake, 33
  Carrot Yogurt Soup, 39
  Fresh Carrot Vinaigrette, 44
Casseroles
  Baked Vegetable and Cream Cheese Casserole, 122

The Cleaned Out The Fridge Casserole, 19
Creamed Leeks, 123
Eggplant Parmesan, 84
Grande Potatoes, 57
Perfect Potatoes, 85
The Spinach Thing, 20
Vegetable Burritos, 51
Zucchini Lasagna, 52
Cauliflower
    Broccoli & Cauliflower Salad Mix, 109
    Cauliflower Soup, 71
    Curried Cauliflower and Spinach, 116
Chard, Swiss
    Paul's Ravioli, 4
    Soul Food Arabe, 120
Cherries
    Cherries Cointreau, 153
Chicken
    Chicken Breast / Snow Pea Stir Fry, 17
    Chicken Sebastopol, 78
    Jambalaya, 75
    Johnson's Chicken with Orange, 113
    Leeky Chicken, 111
    Moo-Goo-Gay-Pan, 112

    Plum Lemon Ginger Chicken Wings, 114
Chocolate
    Chocolate Walnut Fudge, 35
Chutney
    Fuyu Persimmon Chutney, 149
Cookies
    Oatmeal Cookies, 34
    Oatmeal Jam Squares, 130
    Nut and Graham Cracker Goodies, 134
Cucumbers See also Pickles
    Cucumber Salad, 44
Desserts and Baked Goods
see also Cakes, Cookies, Pies, Ice Cream
    Avocado Chiffon Mousse, 32
    Chilled Strawberry Soup, 29
    Cheesecake with Kiwifruit, 97
    Chocolate Walnut Fudge, 35
    Frozen Melon-Orange, 139
    Golden Cottage Pudding, 133
    Lemon Mousse w/Butter Pecan Crust, 129
    Mellow Melon, 63
    Nut and Graham Cracker Goodies, 134
    Peach Crisp, 64

    Pears in Red Wine, 65
    Persimmon Cup, 98
    Raspberry - Tarte Squares, 62
    Rhubarb Crisp, 28
    Sour Apricot & Raspberry Buckle, 67
    Strawberry Rhubarb Frozen Pie, 29
    Sunshine Bars, 30
    Watermelon Sherbet, 66
    Zwetschgendatschi (German Prune Pastry), 101
Dressings   12, 42, 43, 44, 109
    Classic Vinaigrette Dressing, 108
    French Salad Dressing, 10
Eggplant
    Eggplant Florentine, 58
    Eggplant Parmesan, 84
    Eggplant Soup, 41
    Mushroom, Leek and Eggplant Soup, 105
Farmers Markets, about them   2
Fish
    Barbecued Salmon Fillets, 48
    Fillet of Sole Sorreltine, 18
    Fish Fillets with Spinach, Chard or Sorrel, 47
    Salmon Saute in Blue Cornmeal, 49
    Quenelles of Salmon, 50

Red Snapper Fillet with Greenhouse
  Greens, 115
Fruit. *See* individual fruits
Fruit Butters *See also* Jams and Jellies
  Apple Butter, 156
  Nectarine Butter, 156
Fruit Salads
  Cabbage-Apple Slaw, 74
  Fruit Salad, 74
  Mellow Melon, 63
  Summer Fruit Salad with Honey-Lime
  Dressing, 43
Gnocchi, 25
Grapes
  Christmas Grapes, 155
Greens
  Anise Greens Soup, 40
  Kiwi and Spinach Salad, 107
  Mustard Greens with Raspberry Vine-
  gar, 21
  Red Snapper Fillet with Greenhouse
  Greens, 115
  Spinach and Ricotta Gnocchi, 25
  Turnip Greens Soup, 40
Ice Cream
  Kiwi Freezer Ice Cream, 93
Jambalaya, 75

Jams and Jellies *See also* Chutney
  Apple Butter, 156
  Kiwi Pineapple Jam, 151
  Nectarine Butter, 156
  Peach-Orange Preserves, 151
  Sweet Pepper Jam Appetizer, 150
  Spicy Pepper Jam, 150
Kale
  Red Bean and Kale Soup, 9
Kiwifruit
  Cheesecake with Kiwifruit, 97
  Kiwi Freezer Ice Cream, 93
  Kiwi and Spinach Salad, 107
  Kiwi-Pineapple Jam, 151
  Spicy Kiwi Meat Sauce, 90
Kohlrabi
  Stuffed Kohlrabi, 23
Lamb
  Glazed Lamb Chops, 16
  Grilled Sonoma Lamb Chops with
  Bagnat, 46
  Lamb Wellington, 14
  Rack of Lamb with Herbs, 15
Leeks
  Creamed Leeks, 123
  Leeky Chicken, 111
  Mushroom, Leek and Eggplant

Soup, 105
  Potato-Leek Soup, 106
Lemons
  Lemon Chiffon Cake, 31
  Preserved Lemons, 154
Limes
  Key Lime Cake, 127
Marinades 48, 76, 77
Meats. *See* Beef; Chicken; Lamb; Pork;
  Rabbit; Turkey; Veal
Melons
  Frozen Melon-Orange, 139
  Mellow Melon, 63
  Watermelon Sherbet, 66
Mushrooms
  Mushroom Bisque, 8
  Mushroom, Leek and Eggplant Soup,
  105
  Quick Harvest Dinner, 83
  Sauteed Mushrooms, 48
Mustard Greens. *See* Greens
Nectarines
  Nectarine Butter, 156
Noodles. *See* Pasta
Nuts
  Chocolate Walnut Fudge, 35

Nut and Graham Cracker Goodies,134
Pecan Pie, 100
Oatmeal
  Oatmeal Cookies, 34
  Oatmeal Jam Squares, 130
  Oatmeal Raisin Bread, 27
Onions *See also* Leeks
  French Onion Soup, 72
Oranges
  Peach-Orange Preserves, 151
Parsley, 139
Pasta and Noodles
  Noodles and Cabbage, 21
  Pasta a la Oje, 119
  Paul's Ravioli, 4
  Pumpkin Raviolis with Brie Nutmeg
  Cream, 79
Pastry
  Pate Brisee, 26
  Plain Pastry, 94
Peaches
  Peach Crisp, 64
  Peach-Orange Preserves, 151
Pears
  Pears in Red Wine, 65
Peas, Snow
  Chicken Breast /Snow Pea Stir Fry,17

Pecans. *See* Nuts
Peppers, Red and Green Bell, 139
  Baked Green Peppers with Feta, To-
  mato and Walnuts, 87
  Spicy Pepper Jam, 150
  Sweet Pepper Jam Appetizer, 150
  Sweet Red Bell Pepper Soup, 73
Peppers, Jalapeno
  Spicy Pepper Jam, 150
  Two Broads Knock-Your-Socks-Off
  Salsa, 88
Persimmons
  Fuyu Persimmon Chutney, 149
  Persimmon Cup, 98
  Persimmon Pudding, 96
Pickles & Pickling
  Bread and Butter Pickles, 142
  Dill Pickles, 140
  Green Pickle Relish, 143
  Jennifer's Pickled Jerusalem Arti-
  chokes, 141
  Yellow Crookneck Squash Relish,
  145
  Zucchini Relish, 144
Pies
  Broccoli Pie, 118
  Butternut Squash Pie, 94

Lemon Mousse with Butter Pecan
  Crust   129
Mustard Tart, 26
Pecan Pie   100
Strawberry Rhubarb Frozen Pie   29
Zucchini Pie, 55
Pistachios
  Vanilla Pistachio Cake, 132
Plums
  Plums for A.J., 152
Polenta
  Grilled Polenta with Fontina Cheese &
  Shiitake Mushrooms, 56
Potatoes
  Grande Potatoes, 57
  Potato-Leek Soup, 106
  Potato Pancakes, 80
  Perfect Potatoes, 85
  Tiny New Potatoes w/Fresh Herbs, 22
Preserves. *See also* Chutney, Jams &
  Jellies, Pickles, Relishes
  Apricot Sundaes, 149
  Cherries Cointreau, 153
  Christmas Grapes, 155
  Peach-Orange Preserves, 151
  Plums for A.J., 152
  Preserved Lemons, 154

160

Prunes
    Prune Cake, 99
    Zwetschgendatschi (German Prune
    Pastry), 101
Pudding
    Persimmon Cup, 98
    Persimmon Pudding, 96
Pumpkin
    Pumpkin Bread, 91
    Pumpkin Ravioli, 79
Quiches
    Alicia's Quiche, 24
Rabbit
    Lapin Gravenstein, 45
Raspberries
    Raspberry Bread, 60
    Raspberry - Tarte Squares, 62
    Sour Apricot & Raspberry Buckle, 67
Relishes
    Green Pickle Relish, 143
    Yellow Crookneck Squash Relish,
    145
    Zucchini Relish, 144
Rhubarb
    Rhubarb Crisp, 28
    Strawberry Rhubarb Frozen Pie, 29

Rice
    Jambalaya, 75
    Quick Harvest Dinner, 83
    Wild Rice Salad, 42
Roux, 8
Salad Dressings. *See* Dressings
Salads
    Broccoli Salad, 109
    Broccoli & Cauliflower Salad Mix, 109
    Crisp Sorrel Salad, 11
    Cucumber Salad, 44
    Fresh Carrot Vinaigrette, 44
    Fresh Green Salad, 12
    Spinach Salad, California Style, 108
    Wild Rice Salad, 42
Salsa
    Corn and Red Pepper Salsa, 76
    Salsa Cruda, 50
    Two Broads Knock-Your-Socks-Off
    Salsa, 88
Sauces *see also* Dressings, Salsa
    Bearnaise Sauce, 59
    Fast Spaghetti Sauce, 89
    Italian Marinara Sauce, 89
    Raspberry Hollandaise, 124
    Sauce Vin Blanc, 50
    Sauce Vinaigrette, 10

    Sauce for Leftover Meats, 90
    Sauce for Sauteed Vegies, 124
    Spicy Kiwi Meat Sauce, 90
Sorrel
    Crisp Sorrel Salad, 11
    Fillet of Sole Sorreltine, 18
    Fish Fillets with Spinach, Chard or
    Sorrel, 47
    Sorrel Soup, 104
Soups
    Anise Greens Soup, 40
    Cabbage Borsht, 70
    Carrot Yogurt Soup, 39
    Cauliflower Soup, 71
    Chilled Strawberry Soup, 29
    Eggplant Soup, 41
    Fava Bean Soup, 9
    French Onion Soup, 72
    Giant Zucchini Soup, 38
    Mushroom Bisque, 8
    Mushroom, Leek and Eggplant
     Soup, 105
    Potato-Leek Soup, 106
    Red Bean and Kale Soup, 9
    Sorrel Soup, 104
    Sweet Red Bell Pepper Soup, 73
    Turnip Greens Soup, 40

Spinach
    Curried Cauliflower and Spinach, 116
    Fish Fillets with Spinach, Chard or
    Sorrel, 47
    Kiwi and Spinach Salad, 107
    Spinach and Ricotta Gnocchi, 25
    Spinach Salad, California Style, 108
    The Spinach Thing, 20
    Spinach Timbales, 121
Squash
    Butternut Squash Pie, 94
    Squash Patties, 117
    Yellow Crookneck Squash Relish,
    145
Strawberries
    Chilled Strawberry Soup, 29
    Strawberry Rhubarb Frozen Pie, 29
Sunchokes. *See* Artichokes, Jerusalem
Tomatoes
    Auntie Ann's Ketchup, 146
    Tomato Sauce, 147
    Two Broads Knock-Your-Socks-Off
    Salsa, 88
Turkey
    Fiesta Sonoma Grilled Turkey, 77
Veal
    Mesquite Grilled Veal Loin w/ Baby

Vegetable Ragout, 76
Vinegars, Herb 138
Walnuts. *See* Nuts
Watermelons. *See* Melons
Wine 29, 50, 65, 77, 135
Zucchini
    Giant Zucchini Soup, 38
    Stuffed Zucchini, 53
    Zucchini Bread, 61
    Zucchini Lasagna, 52
    Zucchini Pancakes, 54
    Zucchini Pie, 55
    Zucchini Relish, 144